Decisions
of the
United States
Supreme Court

1964-65 TERM
---

by
The Editorial Staff
United States Supreme Court Reports,
Lawyers' Edition

The Lawyers Co-operative Publishing Company
Rochester, New York

Library of Congress Catalog Card Number: 64-17924

PREFACE

This volume is designed to serve as a quick-reference guide to the work of the United States Supreme Court during its 1964–1965 Term. Its important features are described below.

The Court's Personnel. A list of the operating personnel of the Court is accompanied by photographs and biographical sketches of each Justice serving during the Term.

Survey of the Term. A succinct narrative statement outlines the high spots of the Term.

Summaries of Decisions. Each decision of the Supreme Court in which a written opinion was issued is individually summarized. These Summaries describe the manner in which the case came before the Court, the facts involved and issues presented, the holding of the Court and the reasons supporting that holding, the name of the Justice who wrote the opinion of the majority, and the names and views of those of the Justices who concurred or dissented.

The Summaries are printed in the order in which the cases were decided by the Court. Notations to each Summary indicate the volume and page at which the full opinion of the Court may be found in the official reports (US) published by the federal government, and the privately published United States Supreme Court Reports, Lawyers Edition (L ed 2d), and Supreme Court Reporter (S Ct).

Following each Summary is a listing of the attorneys who acted in behalf of the litigants.

Glossary. A glossary of common legal terms defines, in laymen's language, various legal words and phrases used in the Supreme Court's decisions and in the Summaries of those decisions that appear in this volume.

Table of Cases. A complete Table of Cases makes possible the location of the Summary of any case through the name of a party litigant.

Index. A detailed, alphabetical word index makes possible the location of the Summary of any case by consulting the index entries for appropriate factual and conceptual terms.

THE COURT'S PERSONNEL

JUSTICES

OF THE

SUPREME COURT OF THE UNITED STATES

––––––––––

1964–1965 Term

––––––––––

Chief Justice
HON. EARL WARREN

Associate Justices
HON. HUGO L. BLACK

HON. WILLIAM O. DOUGLAS

HON. TOM C. CLARK

HON. JOHN M. HARLAN

HON. WILLIAM J. BRENNAN, Jr.

HON. POTTER STEWART

HON. BYRON R. WHITE

HON. ARTHUR J. GOLDBERG

BIOGRAPHIES OF THE
JUSTICES

Mr. Chief Justice Warren was born in Los Angeles, California, on March 19, 1891, the son of Methias H. and Chrystal (Hernlund) Warren. He married Nina E.  Meyers on October 14, 1925. They have six children, James C., Virginia (Mrs. John Charles Daly), Earl, Dorothy (Mrs. Carmine Clemente), Nina Elizabeth (Mrs. Stuart Brien), and Robert.

Mr. Chief Justice Warren attended the public schools of Bakersfield, and graduated from the University of California in 1912 with a B.L. degree, and from the School of Jurisprudence of the University of California in 1914 with a J.D. degree. After admission to the California Bar in 1914, he engaged in private law practice in San Francisco and Oakland until 1917.

He enlisted in the United States Army as a private in 1917, and was discharged as a First Lieutenant in 1918, having attained the rank of Captain as a member of the Reserve Corps from 1919 to 1935.

Mr. Chief Justice Warren was Clerk of the Assembly Judiciary Committee of the California Legislature in 1919, and served as Deputy City Attorney of Oakland from 1919 to 1920. From 1920 to 1925, he was Deputy District Attorney of Alameda County, and from 1925 to 1939 he was District Attorney of Alameda County. After serving as Attorney General of California from 1939 to 1943, Mr. Chief Justice Warren became Governor of California, serving from 1943 to October, 1953. He was the Republican nominee for Vice President of the United States in 1948.

Mr. Chief Justice Warren was nominated Chief Justice of the United States by President Eisenhower and took his seat on October 5, 1953.

Mr. Chief Justice Warren is a member of the State Bar of California, the Alameda County Bar Association, and the Sacramento County Bar Association. He was president of the National Association of Attorneys General from 1940 to 1941.

Included among the important public functions performed by Mr. Chief Justice Warren in his period of service on the high court has been leadership of the Warren Commission, appointed by President Johnson to investigate and report to the American people on the assassination of President John F. Kennedy.

Mr. Justice Black was born in Harlan, Alabama, on February 27, 1886, the son of William LaFayette and Martha Ardellah (Toland) Black.  In 1921 he married Josephine Patterson Foster, who died December 7, 1952. They had three children, Hugo, Jr., Sterling Foster, and Martha Josephine (Mrs. Mario Pesaresi). On September 11, 1957, he married Mrs. Elizabeth Seay DeMeritte.

Mr. Justice Black was educated in the public schools of Ashland, Alabama. After completing a two-year medical course at the University of Alabama in Birmingham, he entered the study of law and received his LL.B. from the University of Alabama Law School in 1906.

Mr. Justice Black entered private practice in Ashland in 1907, and later moved his practice to Birmingham. In 1910 and 1911 he served as a police judge, and from 1915 to 1917 he served as prosecuting attorney for Jefferson County, Alabama. In 1917 he entered Officers' Training School at Fort Oglethorpe, Georgia. During World War I he served as Captain in the 81st Field Artillery and as Adjutant in the 19th Artillery Brigade. After the war he entered the general practice of law in Birmingham. He was elected to the United States Senate in 1926, where he served two terms.

Mr. Justice Black was appointed to the position of Associate Justice of the United States Supreme Court by President Franklin D. Roosevelt on August 12, 1937.

Mr. Justice Douglas was born in Maine, Minnesota, on October 16, 1898. His father was William Douglas, and his mother was Julia Bickford Fisk. Mr. Justice Douglas has a daughter, Mrs. Frank Wells, Jr., and a son, William O. Douglas, Jr.

He attended grade and high schools in Yakima, Washington, and received his A.B. from Whitman College, Walla Walla, in 1920, and his LL.B. from Columbia Law School in New York in 1925.

In 1918, Mr. Justice Douglas served as a private in the United States Army (SATC).

Mr. Justice Douglas was a member of the faculty of the Columbia Law School from 1924 to 1928, and the Yale Law School from 1928 to 1936. He served as Commissioner of the Securities and Exchange Commission from 1936 to 1939, and as Chairman of the Securities and Exchange Commission from 1937 to 1939.

Mr. Justice Douglas was nominated by President Roosevelt to be an Associate Justice of the Supreme Court of the United States, and took his seat on April 17, 1939.

Mr. Justice Clark was born in Dallas, Texas, on September 23, 1899, the son of William H. and Jennie (Falls) Clark. On November 8, 1924, he married Mary Ramsey.

They have three children, William Ramsey, Mildred (Mrs. Thomas R. Gronlund), and Tom C., Jr. (deceased).

After his primary education in the public schools of Dallas, he attended the Virginia Military Institute in 1917 and 1918, from which he entered World War I, serving in the 153rd Infantry. In 1919, he entered the University of Texas, receiving his A.B. degree in 1921, and his LL.B. in 1922.

Admitted to the Texas Bar in June, 1922, Mr. Justice Clark became associated with the firm of Clark and Clark, the members being his father and brother. He remained with that firm until 1927, when he became Civil District Attorney for Dallas County. From 1933 to 1935 he was associated in the firm of McCraw and Clark of Dallas. In 1937, Mr. Justice Clark joined the Department of Justice as an attorney, and during the next eight years he served in that Department. In June, 1945, he became Attorney General.

Mr. Justice Clark was nominated Associate Justice of the United States Supreme Court by President Truman on August 2, 1949, and took his seat on October 3, 1949.

The professional organizations of which Mr. Justice Clark is a member include the American, Texas, and Federal Bar Associations (President, 1944 to 1945), the Institute of Judicial Administration, the American College of Trial Lawyers, the American Judicature Society (Board of Directors 1958 to 1959), the National Conference of State Trial Judges, and the National Lawyers Club.

Mr. Justice Harlan was born in Chicago, Illinois, on May 20, 1899, the son of John Maynard and Elizabeth Palmer (Flagg) Harlan. He married Ethel Andrews  on November 10, 1928. They have one daughter, Eve Harlan Newcomb (Mrs. W. A. Newcomb).

After attending Chicago Latin School, Appleby School, and Lake Placid School, Mr. Justice Harlan graduated from Princeton University in 1920 with an A.B. degree. He attended Balliol College from 1921 to 1923 as a Rhodes Scholar, receiving a B.A. degree in Jurisprudence and an M.A. degree. Upon returning from Oxford, Mr. Justice Harlan attended New York Law School and received an LL.B. degree in 1924.

Mr. Justice Harlan was admitted to the New York Bar in 1925. He joined the firm of Root, Clark, Buckner & Howland, subsequently (Root, Ballantine, Harlan, Bushby & Palmer) as an associate in 1923, and was a member of the firm from 1931 to 1954. He served as Assistant U. S. Attorney for the Southern District of New York from 1925 to 1927, and was appointed to the United States Court of Appeals for the Second Circuit in 1954.

He was a Colonel in the United States Army Air Force from 1943 to 1945, serving as Chief of Operations Analysis Section Eighth Air Force, and as a member of Planning Section for the Occupation of Germany, U. S. Strategic Air Forces in Europe.

Mr. Justice Harlan was appointed to the Supreme Court of the United States by President Eisenhower on March 17, 1955, and took office on March 28, 1955.

Mr. Justice Harlan is a member of the American Bar

Association, the New York State Bar Association, the
Association of the Bar of the City of New York, the New
York County Lawyers Association (Director, 1938 to
1942), the American Law Institute, and the National
Legal Aid Association (Director).

Mr. Justice Brennan was born in Newark, New Jersey, on April 25, 1906, the son of William Joseph Brennan, Sr. and Agnes (McDermott) Brennan. He married Mar-

jorie Leonard on May 5, 1928. They have three children, William Joseph Brennan III, Hugh Leonard Brennan, and Nancy Brennan.

Mr. Justice Brennan attended public schools in Newark, and graduated from the University of Pennsylvania in 1928 with a B.S. degree. He earned his LL.B. degree from Harvard University in 1931.

Mr. Justice Brennan was admitted to the New Jersey Bar in 1932, after joining the Newark law firm of Pitney, Hardin & Skinner. Following that, for 10 years, he practiced law in Newark.

In March, 1942, he entered the Army as a Major in the legal division of the Ordnance Department, leaving with the rank of Colonel in September, 1945.

Returning to Newark, he rejoined his law firm and became a name partner in Pitney, Hardin, Ward & Brennan. In 1949 he became a trial judge in the New Jersey Superior Court. After two years he was elevated to a judgeship in the Appellate Division of the same court, and in March, 1952, he was appointed as an Associate Justice of the New Jersey Supreme Court.

President Eisenhower appointed him an Associate Justice of the United States Supreme Court on October 15, 1956, and he took his seat on the Court on October 16, 1956.

Mr. Justice Brennan is a member of the American, New Jersey, Essex County, Hudson County and Monmouth County (N.J.) Bar Associations.

Mr. Justice Stewart was born in Jackson, Michigan, on January 23, 1915, the son of James Garfield Stewart and Harriet Loomis Potter Stewart. He married Mary Ann Bertles on April 24, 1943. They have a daughter, Harriet Potter Stewart, and two sons, Potter Stewart, Jr., and David Bertles Stewart.

After attending the public schools of Cincinnati, Mr. Justice Stewart attended Hotchkiss School and Yale College, receiving in 1937 a B.A. degree, cum laude. He also attended Cambridge University, England, on a Henry Fellowship, and Yale Law School, receiving an LL.B. degree, cum laude, in 1941.

Mr. Justice Stewart was admitted to the Ohio Bar in 1941, and to the New York Bar in 1942. He was an associate in the firm of Debevoise, Stevenson, Plimpton & Page in New York City from 1941 to 1942, and from 1945 to 1947. Mr. Justice Stewart was an associate in the firm of Dinsmore, Shohl, Sawyer & Dinsmore in Cincinnati, Ohio, in 1947, and was a partner of that firm from 1951 to 1954. He was a member of the Cincinnati City Council from 1950 to 1953, and was Vice Mayor of Cincinnati from 1952 to 1953. Mr. Justice Stewart was appointed to the United States Court of Appeals for the Sixth Circuit in 1954.

He volunteered in the United States Naval Reserve in 1941, and was called into active service in 1942. After serving three years active sea duty, he was honorably discharged as a Lieutenant in 1945.

Mr. Justice Stewart was appointed by President Eisenhower as an Associate Justice of the Supreme Court of the United States on October 14, 1958, during a recess of the Senate, and took his oath of office and his seat on that day. He was nominated as an Associate Justice of the Supreme Court by President Eisenhower on January 17, 1959, was confirmed by the Senate on May 5, 1959, and took the oath of office on May 15, 1959.

Mr. Justice Stewart is a member of the American, Ohio, Cincinnati, and City of New York Bar Associations, the American Law Institute, and the American Judicature Society.

Mr. Justice White was born in Ft. Collins, Colorado, on June 8, 1917, the son of Alpha Albert White and Maud Burger White. He married Marion Lloyd Stearns on

June 15, 1946. They have two children, Charles Byron and Nancy Pitkin.

Mr. Justice White attended elementary and high schools at Wellington, Colorado. He graduated from the University of Colorado in 1938 with a B.A. degree, and attended Oxford University, Oxford, England, as a Rhodes Scholar, from January, 1939 until October, 1939. From October, 1939 to October, 1941, and from February, 1946 to November, 1946, he attended Yale University Law School, receiving an LL.B. degree, magna cum laude.

Mr. Justice White volunteered for services in the United States Navy in July 1941 and received a commission as an ensign. During World War II, he served in the Pacific as an intelligence officer, and was honorably discharged as a Lieutenant Commander in 1946.

Upon graduation from Yale, Mr. Justice White served from 1946 to 1947 as law clerk to Chief Justice Vinson, Supreme Court of the United States.

In 1947, he joined the law firm of Lewis, Grant, Newton, Davis and Henry (now Lewis, Grant and Davis), in Denver, Colorado. He became a partner and remained with that firm until January 1961, when he was appointed Deputy Attorney General of the United States by President Kennedy.

Mr. Justice White was nominated by President Kennedy as Associate Justice of the Supreme Court of the United States on April 3, 1962, and took his seat on April 16, 1962.

Mr. Justice Goldberg was born in Chicago, Illinois, on August 8, 1908, the son of Joseph and Rebecca Goldberg.

He married Dorothy Kurgans in 1931. They have two children, a daughter, Barbara Cramer, and a son, Robert M. Goldberg.

After receiving his elementary education in the public schools of Chicago, and after graduating from Benjamin Harrison High School, Mr. Justice Goldberg attended Crane Junior College, a branch of the City College of Chicago. He received a Bachelor of Science in Law degree in 1929, and a Doctor of Jurisprudence degree in 1930, at Northwestern University.

Mr. Justice Goldberg was admitted to practice before the Illinois Bar in 1929 and qualified for practice before the United States Supreme Court in 1937. He was engaged in private law practice in Chicago from 1929 to 1948, and was a member of the firm of Goldberg, Devoe, Shadur & Mikva in Chicago from 1945 to 1961. He practiced law with the firm of Goldberg, Feller & Bredhoff in Washington, D. C., from 1952 to 1961. Mr. Justice Goldberg was Secretary of Labor from 1961 to 1962.

During World War II, he served as special assistant to the Office of Strategic Services, with ranks of Captain and Major.

Mr. Justice Goldberg was appointed as Associate Justice of the United States Supreme Court by President Kennedy on August 29, 1962, and took his seat on October 1, 1962.

SURVEY OF THE 1964–1965 TERM

During the October Term, 1964, which began October 5, 1964 and ended June 7, 1965, the Supreme Court of the United States rendered 111 decisions explained in full opinions of the Court. Most of these cases (72 cases, or about 65% of the total of opinion cases) originated in the lower federal courts, the remaining thirty-six cases arose in the state courts. Of these 108 cases coming from lower federal courts and state courts, 82 were heard on writs of certiorari and 26 on appeals. Three other cases were instituted in the Supreme Court itself.

Administrative law and procedure questions were presented in a number of cases. The Court held that natural gas sales were within the Federal Power Commission's jurisdiction where the gas was contractually restricted to intrastate use but part of it was in fact resold in interstate commerce as a result of commingling with other gas [see pp. 46, 85]. The Federal Power Commission was also held to have jurisdiction over the sale of leasehold interests in a natural gas field [see p. 213].

In other administrative law cases, the Federal Communications Commission was held empowered to require the disclosure in a public hearing of evidence as to television program producing and packaging [see p. 203]; the Federal Reserve Board rather than a lower federal court was held to have jurisdiction to decide a controversy between state-chartered banks and a national bank regarding a plan to create new national banks operated by a bank holding company [see p. 51]; the Secretary of the Interior's reasonable interpretation of an executive order and a public land order as not barring oil and gas leases on certain public lands was held entitled to credence by the courts [see p. 87]; a deputy workmen's compensation commissioner's finding that the drowning of a private employee on a South Korean lake during a Saturday outing arose out of and in the course of employment was held improperly reversed [see p. 128]; the Federal Power Act was held to require the licensing of a hydroelectric power project which utilizes the nonnavigable headwaters of a navigable river to generate energy for an interstate power system, even if commerce on navigable waters is not significantly affected [see p. 186]; and all-commodity railroad freight rates were held not subject to an Interstate Commerce Act provision dealing with class rates [see p. 42].

In the field of **antitrust law,** the Court held that the exemption of certain labor union activities from the antitrust laws did not preclude union liability for entering into an agreement with the larger employers in the coal mining industry to impose uniform labor standards on all employers in the industry [see p. 228], but that a butchers' union did not violate the antitrust laws by obtaining from food retailers an agreement restricting meat marketing hours [see p. 230].

The acquisition by a large food concern of a company commanding a substantial share of the dehydrated onion and garlic market was held to violate the Clayton Act [see p. 161]. Railroad officers who agreed to assist another corporation to obtain profits by purchasing the railroad's coaches, and who received substantial sums from the purchasing corporation pursuant to the agreement, were held not to have a "substantial interest" in the purchasing corporation, within the meaning of prohibitory provisions of the antitrust laws [see p. 105].

Several **apportionment** cases were argued during the Term. The Court upheld a Georgia statute providing for the countywide election of state senators in counties having more than one senator [see p. 54]. It vacated a lower federal court order refusing to stay proceedings in an Illinois legislative apportionment case after the Supreme Court of Illinois had declared an Illinois apportionment scheme invalid and had retained jurisdiction of the case [see p. 216]. After the Idaho legislature adopted a new reapportionment plan, the Court dismissed an appeal from a lower federal court's expired order staying a suit challenging the legislative apportionment [see p. 215]. After a new legislature was elected in Georgia, the Court vacated a lower federal court order enjoining the proposal of a new state constitution by the legislature [see p. 75]. Each of these holdings had as its foundation the rule, established by a series of decisions handed down by the Court in 1964, that seats in a state bicameral legislature must be apportioned on a population basis.

On the other hand, the Court granted a motion by all the parties in a Vermont legislative apportionment case to affirm a lower federal court apportionment decree as modified by a provision permitting the lower court to reapportion the legislature if reapportionment should not otherwise be effected by a certain date [see p. 44]. And despite a New York Court of Appeals judgment invalidating a state legislative apportionment scheme on state grounds, it refused to stay a lower federal court order that the next state election proceed under that scheme [see p. 217].

In cases dealing with **civil procedure,** the Court held that in a civil action brought in federal court because of diversity of citizenship of the parties, Federal Civil Procedure Rule 4(d)(1) rather than state law applies with respect to service of process on an individual [see p. 144]. A divorced father's constitutional rights were held violated by the failure to give him notice of a pending proceeding for the adoption of his child [see p. 154].

Federal Civil Procedure Rule 35, dealing with the physical and mental examination of a "party" in a civil action, and usually invoked to permit the examination of a plaintiff's injuries, was held to permit examination of a defendant under appropriate circumstances [see p. 15]. The Court also held that a prevailing party's expenses for transportating from Saudi Arabia witnesses to testify at a trial in New York and for daily transcripts of the trial record were properly disallowed by the trial court [see p. 29].

With respect to the effect of subsequent statutory changes on the Supreme Court's review of state decisions, the Court vacated an Alaska judgment affirming the dismissal of teachers for "immorality" where the statutory definition of that term was changed after the Alaska court's decision [see p. 190]. Similarly, the Court vacated a Nebraska judgment holding habeas corpus unavailable to vindicate a state prisoner's constitutional claims, sending the case back to the state court for reconsideration in light of a subsequent Nebraska statute providing for postconviction procedure [see p. 209].

With respect to **civil rights,** the Court not only upheld sections of the public accommodations title of the Civil Rights Act of 1964 [see pp. 32, 35] but also held that trespass criminal prosecutions for conduct which occurred prior to its enactment were, in effect, nullified by the statute [see pp. 37, 83]. A Louisiana conviction of a civil rights leader for breach of the peace and obstructing public passages was held unconstitutional as abridging freedom of speech and assembly [see p. 68]; a Louisiana conviction for picketing near a courthouse was held to violate the due process of law guaranteed by the Constitution where officials gave their permission for the picketing [see p. 71].

The Court held unconstitutional a Florida statute making it a criminal offense for a white person and a Negro of opposite sexes to habitually live in the same room [see p. 25].

Several **criminal law and procedure** cases were decided during the Term. The Court held that an accused's right to confront the witnesses against him, guaranteed by the Sixth Amendment to persons charged with crime in a federal court, was also guaranteed to defendants in state criminal prosecutions by the Fourteenth Amendment [see p. 132]. It further held that this right of confrontation was violated when a state prosecutor read the confession of the accused's accomplice who had invoked the privilege against self-incrimination [see p. 134].

The Court upheld Federal Criminal Procedure Rule 23(a), conditioning an accused's waiver of a jury trial upon the trial court's approval and the government's consent [see p. 89].

A much publicized financier was held denied his constitutional rights when his state trial, an affair of great notoriety, was televised and broadcast over his objection [see p. 222]. The constitutional rights of an accused in a state murder prosecution were held violated by the association, during the trial, between jurors and deputy sheriffs who were key prosecution witnesses [see p. 59]. Comments about an accused's failure to testify, made by the prosecuting attorney and the court in a state trial, were held to violate his constitutional rights [see p. 163]. A trial judge's statement in a federal prosecution that the jury must reach a verdict was held to require a new trial because of its coercive effect on the jury [see p. 140].

In another criminal case, a state prisoner was held entitled only to a hearing in state courts, and not to a new trial, on the issue of the voluntariness of his confession introduced at his trial over his objection and without a hearing [see p. 192].

In cases involving **elections,** the Court struck down as

unconstitutional (1) a Louisiana voting registration test requiring applicants to interpret the federal and Louisiana constitutions to the satisfaction of voting registrars [see p. 101], (2) a provision of the Texas constitution denying voting rights to servicemen who moved their homes to Texas during the course of military duty and remained in the armed forces [see p. 97], and a Virginia statute which required either paying a poll tax or filing a certificate of residence as a prerequisite to voting in federal elections [see p. 152]. The Court upheld a federal statute permitting suits by the United States to protect the voting rights of Negroes [see p. 103].

In regard to **freedom of speech,** a federal statute requiring the addressee of mail from abroad containing Communist propaganda material to make a written request for its delivery was held a violation of the addressees' rights of free speech [see p. 205]. A Maryland motion-picture censorship statute was held invalid because of its failure to provide adequate safeguards against undue interference with protected expression [see p. 93].

Other **individual freedoms** were involved in decisions holding unconstitutional, as invading the right of privacy of married persons, a Connecticut statute making the use of contraceptives a criminal offense [see p. 220]; upholding the Secretary of State's refusal to validate passports of United States citizens for travel to Cuba [see p. 176]; and holding that despite their unorthodox beliefs as to a Supreme Being, 3 persons refusing to submit to induction in the armed forces were conscientious objectors exempt from military service [see p. 107].

Several important **labor** decisions were handed down. A provision of the Landrum-Griffin Act making it a crime for a Communist Party member to serve as a union officer or employee was held unconstitutional [see p. 218]. And the Court held that under the National Labor Relations Act, an employer has an absolute right to close his entire business, but not part of his business [see p. 117]. An employer which decided to replace its maintenance employees by employees of an independent contractor was held to have violated its duty to bargain collectively with the union representative of its employees [see p. 27]. The Court also held an employer guilty of an unfair labor practice in discharging employees engaged in union organizational efforts where it relied on a false accusation that they made threats against its property [see p. 1].

In the field of **patents and unfair competition,** the Court held that § 5 of the Federal Trade Commission Act is violated by the undisclosed use of sand-covered plexiglass as "sandpaper" in television commercials demonstrating the moisturizing quality of the advertised shaving cream [see p. 3] and by an agreement between an oil products distributor and a rubber products manufacturer that the distributor, on an overall commission basis, would promote the sale of the manufacturer's products to the distributor's wholesale outlets and retail service station dealers [see p. 211].

With respect to **searches and seizures,** the rule requiring the exclusion of evidence seized in violation of the Fourth Amendment in state criminal trials was held not to apply to cases finally decided before 1961 [see pp. 224, 226], but was held applicable in state proceedings for the forfeiture of an automobile used for the illegal transportation or possession of liquor [see p. 174].

A search warrant was held valid where issued on an affidavit detailing facts observed in all significant respects by government investigators [see p. 99], but a search warrant authorizing the seizure of all literary material concerning the Communist Party of Texas and its operations was held so broad as to be constitutionally intolerable [see p. 61]. Clearinghouse slips obtained in a search incident to an arrest without probable cause were held unlawfully seized and inadmissible in a state criminal prosecution [see p. 13].

In matters directly affecting the **states,** the Court held that Article IV of the Federal Constitution, providing that "Full Faith and Credit shall be given in each State to the public Acts, Records, and judicial Proceedings of every other State," did not preclude Alabama courts from entertaining an Alabama resident's suit against his Georgia employer under the Georgia Workmen's Compensation Act, even though the Georgia statute afforded a remedy only in the Georgia Compensation Board [see p. 91]. The Court also decided a 20-year-old original proceeding involving California's claim to submerged lands off the Pacific Coast, holding that regardless of her claimed historic boundaries, California had title only to those submerged lands shoreward of a line 3 geographical miles from the seaward limit of her "inland waters," and that San Luis Obispo Bay, Santa Barbara Channel, Santa Monica Bay, San Pedro Bay, San Pedro Channel, Newport Bay, and the Gulf of Santa Catalina are not inland waters, while Monterey Bay is inland water [see p. 194].

In a case involving **subversive activities,** the Court struck down as unconstitutionally vague a Louisiana statute making it a felony to participate in the formation or management of "any subversive organization," as defined therein [see p. 146].

Tax cases comprised a significant proportion of the Court's workload during the Term. The Court held that the gain from the sale of discounted, noninterest-bearing notes was taxable as ordinary income rather than as a capital gain even though at the time of the transaction the taxpayers relied on the Commissioner's published acquiescence in a Tax Court decision interpreted by the taxpayers as requiring capital gains treatment, and the acquiescence was subsequently withdrawn retroactively [see p. 182]. Such a gain was also held taxable as ordinary income under the Internal Revenue Code of 1939 [see p. 180]. On the other hand, the transfer of a business to a tax-exempt foundation was held to be a "sale" entitled to capital gains treatment, even though the purchase price was payable in installments out of the future operating profits of the business and the business was leased to a newly formed corporation [see p. 158].

The Court held that a life insurance company was not entitled to deduct from investment income such part of the interest on nontaxable municipal bonds as was allocated to the policyholders' reserve and thus excluded from the company's taxable income [see p. 199]. The statutory sales price fixed in the Merchant Ship Sales Act was held to be the proper cost basis in computing depreciation allowances on vessels purchased from the United States before the effective date of the Act [see p. 201]. In another case, contract coal miners were held not entitled to share with the lessee of coal lands the depletion deduction under the Code [see p. 165].

In two cases, the Court held that the government is not required to show probable cause for suspecting fraud when it begins a proceeding to enforce an administrative summons requiring a taxpayer to testify and to produce records of tax years as to which the 3-year statute of limitations bars assessment of additional deficiencies except for fraud [see pp. 7, 9].

A lower federal court's temporary injunction against a national bank in New York with an Uruguayan branch office, freezing the property of a Uruguay corporation, was held to be a reasonable measure to protect jeopardy tax assessments [see p. 49]. A defendant indicted for income tax evasion in violation of one section of the Internal Revenue Code was held not entitled to instructions concerning other, lesser offenses prohibited by two other Code sections [see p. 124].

In cases not involving federal income taxes, the Court

held that the proceeds of flight insurance were includible in the insured's estate for federal estate tax purposes [see p. 170]. An Idaho excise tax was held unconstitutional as applied to a sale occurring in another state [see p. 142]. An Arizona tax on a trading post's income from sales to Indians on a reservation was held invalid as conflicting with federal statutes [see p. 172]. A regulation of tax commissioners in the District of Columbia, basing the apportionment formula for determining the income of a corporation subject to a local franchise tax exclusively on the sales factor was held unauthorized under the District of Columbia Income and Franchise Tax Act [see p. 156].

In **tort** cases the Court held that the period within which suit must be brought under the Federal Employers' Liability Act is interrupted by a state court action under that statute, notwithstanding the dismissal of the state action because instituted in the wrong state court [see p. 136]. In another Federal Employers' Liability Act case, a state court was held to have improperly invaded the jury's province by overturning, as based on conjecture, a jury verdict for an injured railroad employee [see p. 79]. The Court also held that a civilian and military member of a National Guard unit not in active federal service was not an employee of the United States for the purposes of the Federal Tort Claims Act [see p. 178].

A 1954 **treaty** with Greece was held applicable to a Greek national's claims to recover part of the estate of a person who died in Iowa [see p. 188].

†

SUMMARIES OF DECISIONS

NATIONAL LABOR RELATIONS BOARD,
Petitioner,

v

BURNUP AND SIMS, Inc.

379 US 21, 13 L ed 2d 1, 85 S Ct 171

Argued October 15, 1964. Decided
November 9, 1964.

Decision: Employer held guilty of unfair labor practice
in discharging employees engaged in union organizational efforts on the basis of false accusation that they
made threats against employer's property.

SUMMARY

During a union organizational drive, an employee told
the employer that two employees who undertook to or-
ganize the other employees said that the union would
use dynamite to get in if it did not acquire the author-
izations. The employer discharged the two employees
because of their alleged statements, but in an unfair
labor practice proceeding before the National Labor Relations Board, the Board found that the two employees
had made no threats against the employer's property, and
it ordered the employer to reinstate them with back pay
from the time of their discharge. (137 NLRB 766.)
The United States Court of Appeals for the Fifth Circuit refused reinstatement, holding that since the employer acted in good faith, the discharges were not unlawful. (322 F2d 57.)

On certiorari, the Supreme Court of the United States reversed. In an opinion by **Douglas, J.**, expressing the views of eight members of the Court, it was held that the employer was guilty of an unfair labor practice under § 8(a)(1) of the National Labor Relations Act (29 USC § 158(a)(1)), regardless of its motive, by discharging an employee engaged in a protected activity which the employer knew was such, for an alleged act of misconduct in the course of the activity of which the employee was not guilty.

Harlan, J., concurring in part and dissenting in part, stated that the Court of Appeals' judgment should be vacated and the case remanded to the Board for further proceedings, because reinstatement of a mistakenly discharged employee with back pay is required only as of the time that the employer learned or should have learned of his mistake, subject, however, to a valid business reason for refusing reinstatement.

COUNSEL

Arnold Ordman argued the cause for petitioner. With him on the brief were Solicitor General Cox, Dominick L. Manoli and Norton J. Come.

Erle Phillips argued the cause and filed a brief for respondent.

WALTER C. BRULOTTE et al., Petitioners,

v

THYS COMPANY

379 US 29, 13 L ed 2d 99, 85 S Ct 176

Argued October 20, 1964. Decided
November 16, 1964.

Decision: Patent owner held not entitled to collect royalty
payments accruing after the expiration of patents
incorporated in machines sold to licensees.

SUMMARY

The owner of various patents for hop picking, which
were incorporated in machines sold at flat sums to certain
hop farmers, sued the farmers in the Superior Court of
Yakima County, Washington, to recover royalty payments under licenses issued to each farmer which required
payment of either a minimum royalty per hop-picking
season or an amount calculated on the number of pounds
harvested by the machine, whichever was greater, and
further provided that the licenses could not be assigned
and that the machines could not be removed from Yakima
County. Although all of the patents expired before the
licenses, the Superior Court awarded judgment to the
patent owner for royalty payments accruing after the
expiration of the patents, and the Supreme Court of
Washington affirmed. (62 Wash 2d 284, 382 P2d 271.)

On certiorari, the Supreme Court of the United States
reversed. In an opinion by **Douglas, J.**, expressing the
views of eight members of the Court, it was held that
(1) the use by a patentee of royalty agreements projecting
beyond the expiration date of the patent is unlawful per
se, (2) the provisions for annual payments apart from
the purchase price of the machines, for nonassignment of

the licenses, and for nonremoval of the machines from the county, were a telltale sign that the patent owner was attempting to project his monopoly beyond the patent period, and (3) the judgment would therefore be reversed insofar as it allowed royalties to be collected after the last of the patents had expired.

Harlan, J., dissenting, expressed the view that the judgment should be affirmed because the license agreements contained restrictions less objectionable than other post-expiration use restrictions which are clearly acceptable.

COUNSEL

Edward S. Irons argued the cause for petitioners. With him on the briefs was Charles C. Countryman.

Elwood Hutcheson argued the cause for respondent. With him on the brief was George W. Wilkins.

Solicitor General Cox, Assistant Attorney General Orrick and Robert B. Hummel filed a brief for the United States, as amicus curiae, urging reversal.

Rufus S. Day, Jr., Robert W. Fulwider and Robert J. Woolsey filed a brief for Well Surveys, Inc., as amicus curiae, urging affirmance.

BOLES

v

STEVENSON

379 US 43, 13 L ed 2d 109, 85 S Ct 174

November 16, 1964

Decision: State prisoner held entitled only to a hearing in state courts, and not to a new trial, on the issue of the voluntariness of his confession introduced at his trial over objection and without a hearing.

SUMMARY

During a murder trial in the Common Pleas Court of Cabell County, West Virginia, the accused's oral confession was received in evidence over his objection, without comment by the trial judge and without a hearing as to its voluntariness. The conviction was affirmed on appeal by the West Virginia Supreme Court of Appeals, and certiorari was denied by the Supreme Court of the United States, but in a subsequent habeas corpus proceeding the United States District Court for the Northern District of West Virginia issued a writ of habeas corpus ordering the prisoner's release conditioned on the state's failure to retry him within a reasonable time (221 F Supp 411), and the United States Court of Appeals for the Fourth Circuit affirmed (331 F2d 939).

On certiorari, the Supreme Court of the United States modified the judgment, affirmed it as modified, and remanded the case to the District Court to afford the prisoner either a hearing or a new trial, failing which he was entitled to his release. In a per curiam opinion expressing the views of eight members of the Court, it was held that (1) the writ of habeas corpus properly issued because the record did not show whether the trial judge decided the issue of the voluntariness of the confession, and if so, what standards were relied on, but (2) the prisoner was only entitled to an adequate hearing on the issue of voluntariness.

Black, J., expressed the view that the judgment below, approving the writ as issued, should be affirmed.

COUNSEL

Charles Robert Sarver and Claude A. Joyce, Assistant Attorneys General of West Virginia, for petitioner.
Daniel J. Meador for respondent.

UNITED STATES et al., Petitioners,

v

MAX POWELL et al.

379 US 48, 13 L ed 2d 112, 85 S Ct 248

Argued October 14 and 15, 1964.
Decided November 23, 1964.

Decision: In proceeding to enforce administrative summons requiring taxpayer to testify and produce records of tax years as to which 3-year statute of limitations bars assessment of additional deficiencies except for fraud, government held not required to show probable cause for suspecting fraud.

SUMMARY

The Internal Revenue Service summoned a corporate taxpayer's president in 1963 to give testimony and produce records relating to the taxpayer's 1958 and 1959 returns, but the president refused to produce the records because the 3-year statute of limitations barred assessment of deficiencies for those years except in cases of fraud, and the Service indicated no grounds for its belief that a fraud had been committed. In a subsequent proceeding brought pursuant to § 7604(b) of the 1954 Internal Revenue Code for enforcement of the administrative summons, the United States District Court for the Eastern District of Pennsylvania ruled that an internal revenue agent be given one hour to re-examine the taxpayer's records. The United States Court of Appeals for the Third Circuit reversed on the ground that the examination was an "unnecessary examination," barred by § 7605(b), unless the Service had information which might cause a reasonable man to suspect that there had been fraud in the returns for the closed years, and that whether this was established was to be decided in an adversary proceeding. (325 F2d 914.)

On certiorari, the Supreme Court of the United States reversed. In an opinion by **Harlan, J.**, expressing the views of six members of the Court, it was held that (1) since there was no contumacious refusal by the taxpayer, the enforcement proceeding should have been brought under §§ 7402(b) or 7604(a), rather than § 7604(b), but the proceeding would be deemed brought under the proper sections since the government did not seek the sanctions peculiar to § 7604(b); (2) the government was not required to make a showing of probable cause to suspect fraud; and (3) the taxpayer's defense based on the statute of limitations and on the fact that the records had already been examined was insufficient to sustain its burden of showing an abuse of the court's process.

Douglas, J., joined by **Stewart** and **Goldberg, JJ.**, dissented on the ground that where the limitations period has expired, the Service must overcome a presumption that the examination is unnecessary.

COUNSEL

Bruce J. Terris argued the cause for the United States et al. With him on the briefs were Solicitor General Cox, Assistant Attorney General Oberdorfer, Joseph M. Howard, Meyer Rothwacks and Norman Sepenuk.

Bernard G. Segal argued the cause for respondents. With him on the brief was Samuel D. Slade.

BAYARD EDWARD RYAN, Petitioner,

v

UNITED STATES

379 US 61, 13 L ed 2d 122, 85 S Ct 232

Argued October 14, 1964. Decided
November 23, 1964.

Decision: In proceeding to enforce administrative summons requiring taxpayer to produce records of tax
years as to which 3-year statute of limitations bars
assessment of additional deficiencies except for fraud,
government held not required to show probable cause
for suspecting fraud.

SUMMARY

An internal revenue agent issued a summons to a taxpayer in 1961, ordering him to produce his books for
the years 1942–1953, and when the taxpayer refused
to produce the records on the ground that the tax liability for those years was long since barred except for
fraud, the government instituted an enforcement proceeding in the United States District Court for the Eastern District of Kentucky. The District Court ordered
the taxpayer to produce those records which he had
available, and the United States Court of Appeals for the
Sixth Circuit affirmed on the theory that no full-scale
showing of probable cause need be made. (320 F2d 500.)

On certiorari, the Supreme Court of the United States
affirmed. In an opinion by **Harlan, J.**, expressing the
views of six members of the Court, it was held that (1)
the government was not required to make a showing of
probable cause to suspect fraud, and (2) the taxpayer's
defense based on the statute of limitations was insufficient

to sustain the burden of showing an abuse of the court's process.

Stewart and **Goldberg, JJ.**, concurred in the result on the ground that the agent's testimony constituted a sufficient showing that the government was not proceeding capriciously.

Douglas, J., dissented on the ground that where the limitation period has expired, the Internal Revenue Service must overcome a presumption that the examination is unnecessary.

COUNSEL

William R. Bagby argued the cause and filed briefs for petitioner.

Bruce J. Terris argued the cause for the United States. On the brief were Solicitor General Cox, Acting Assistant Attorney General Jones, Joseph M. Howard and Norman Sepenuk.

JIM GARRISON, Appellant,

v

STATE OF LOUISIANA

379 US 64, 13 L ed 2d 125, 85 S Ct 209

Reargued October 19, 1964. Decided
November 23, 1964.

Decision: Judgment imposing criminal sanctions on district attorney for statements disparaging judicial conduct reversed as in violation of the constitutional guaranty of free speech.

SUMMARY

During a dispute with the judges of the Criminal District Court of the Parish of New Orleans, the district attorney for the parish held a press conference at which he attributed a large backlog of pending criminal cases to the inefficiency, laziness, and excessive vacations of the judges, and accused them of hampering his enforcement of the vice laws by refusing to authorize the expenses for the necessary investigations. He was tried without a jury before a judge from another parish and convicted, in the Criminal District Court of the Parish of New Orleans, of criminal defamation as defined in a Louisiana statute. The Supreme Court of Louisiana affirmed the conviction. (244 La 787, 154 So 2d 400.) The Louisiana Supreme Court interpreted the statute as permitting punishment of truthful criticism of public officials if made with actual malice, and punishment of false statements made with ill will.

On appeal, the United States Supreme Court reversed. In an opinion by **Brennan, J.,** expressing the views of six members of the Court, it was held that (1) the rule announced in New York Times Co. v Sullivan, 376 US 254, 11 L ed 2d 686, 84 S Ct 710, under which the Federal Constitution limits state power, in a civil action brought by a public official for criticism of his official conduct, to an award of damages for a false statement made with actual malice, also limits state power to impose criminal sanctions for such criticism, (2) the district attorney's statement was within the purview of criticism of the official conduct of public officials, entitled to the benefit of the New York Times rule, and (3) the Louisiana defamation statute, as applied in the present case, violated the constitutional guaranties of free speech.

Black, J., joined by Douglas, J., concurred in the result, expressing the view that there is no place for the old, discredited English Star Chamber law of seditious libel.

Douglas, J., joined by Black, J., in a separate concurring opinion, also expressed the view that the constitutional guaranty of free speech prohibits prosecution for seditious libel even for a knowingly false statement or one made with reckless disregard of the truth.

Goldberg, J., concurred in the result on the ground that libel on the official conduct of government officials, as well as libel on government, "has no place in our Constitution."

COUNSEL

Eberhard P. Deutch reargued the cause for appellant. With him on the briefs was Rene H. Himel, Jr.

Jack P. F. Germillion, Attorney General of Louisiana, reargued the cause for appellee. With him on the briefs were M. E. Culligan and John E. Jackson Jr., Assistant Attorneys General.

WILLIAM BECK, Petitioner,

v

STATE OF OHIO

379 US 89, 13 L ed 2d 142, 85 S Ct 223

Argued October 15, 1964. Decided
November 23, 1964.

Decision: 4th and 14th Amendments held violated by arrest without warrant and search of suspect; clearinghouse slips obtained thereby held not admissible as evidence in state prosecution for possession of such slips.

SUMMARY

After defendant's motion to suppress as evidence clearinghouse slips allegedly obtained by an unlawful search of his person following his arrest without warrant had been overruled, he was convicted in the Municipal Court of Cleveland, Ohio, of possession of these slips in violation of an Ohio statute. His conviction was affirmed by an Ohio Court of Appeals, and ultimately by the Supreme Court of Ohio, with two judges dissenting. (175 Ohio St 73, 23 Ohio Ops 2d 377, 191 NE2d 825.)

On certiorari the United States Supreme Court reversed. In an opinion by Stewart, J., expressing the views of six members of the Court, it was held that (1) the record did not support a finding of probable cause for defendant's arrest, (2) the search incident to that arrest violated the Fourth and Fourteenth Amendments, and (3) consequently the slips were not admissible as evidence.

Clark, J., joined by Black, J., dissented on the ground that the record was sufficient to support a finding of probable cause.

Harlan, J., also dissented, expressing the view that the record, while not free from all doubt, was sufficient to carry the day for the state's judgment.

COUNSEL

James R. Willis argued the cause for petitioner. With him on the brief was Jay B. White.

William T. McKnight argued the cause for respondent. With him on the brief was Edward V. Cain.

Bernard A. Berkman and Melvin L. Wulf filed a brief for the American Civil Liberties Union et al., as amici curiae, urging reversal.

John T. Corrigan filed a brief for the County of Cuyahoga, Ohio, as amicus curiae, urging affirmance.

ROBERT L. SCHLAGENHAUF, Petitioner,

v

CALE J. HOLDER, United States District Judge for the Southern District of Indiana

379 US 104, 13 L ed 2d 152, 85 S Ct 234

Argued October 13, 1964. Decided November 23, 1964.

Decision: Federal Civil Procedure Rule 35 held to permit examination of defendant under appropriate circumstances.

SUMMARY

Bus passengers injured when the bus struck a tractor-trailer in the rear sued the bus company, the bus driver, the tractor-trailer owners, and the tractor driver in the United States District Court for the Southern District of Indiana, and the bus company cross-claimed against the tractor-trailer owners. The tractor owner answered, asserting that the bus driver was not mentally or physically capable of driving the bus, and the trailer owner cross-claimed, averring that the bus driver's eyes and vision were impaired and deficient. The tractor-trailer owners also petitioned the court for examination of the bus driver under Federal Civil Procedure Rule 35 by specialists in internal medicine, ophthalmology, neurology, and psychiatry, attaching to their petition an attorney's affidavit that an eyewitness of the accident saw the truck's lights for three-quarters to half of a mile before the impact, and that the bus driver had been involved in a similar previous rear-end collision, and with respect to the accident in suit, had admitted seeing red lights for 10 to 15 seconds before the collision and still drove his bus on without reducing speed and without altering his course. The

District Court ordered the examinations on the basis of the tractor owner's petition and without a hearing. The bus driver then applied to the United States Court of Appeals for the Seventh Circuit for a writ of mandamus setting aside the District Court's order. The application was denied. (321 F2d 43.)

On certiorari, the Supreme Court of the United States vacated the Court of Appeals' judgment and remanded the case to the District Court. In an opinion by **Goldberg, J.**, expressing the views of five members of the Court, it was held that (1) the Court of Appeals had power to review on a petition for mandamus the basic, undecided question whether a District Court can order the mental or physical examination of a defendant; (2) Rule 35 is constitutional and within the scope of the Rules Enabling Act; (3) a Federal District Court has power to order the examination of a party defendant under Rule 35, even on the application of a codefendant, but lacks power to order examination of nonparties; and (4) the tractor-trailer owners failed to make the necessary showing that the bus driver's physical or mental condition was "in controversy" or that "good cause" was shown for the examination, as required by Rule 35.

Black, J., joined by **Clark, J.**, concurring in part and dissenting in part, stated that as to (4) above, the record showed that the bus driver's condition was "in controversy" and that "good cause" was shown for an examination.

Douglas, J., dissenting in part, stated that he would deny all relief under Rule 35 on the ground that the Rule does not permit examination of defendants in negligence suits.

Harlan, J., dissented on the ground that mandamus did not lie to determine the application of the "in controversy" and "good cause" requirements of Rule 35.

COUNSEL

Robert S. Smith argued the cause for petitioner. With him on the briefs was Wilbert McInerney.

Erle A. Kightlinger argued the cause for respondent. With him on the brief were Aribert L. Young and Keith C. Reese.

JESSE M. CALHOON, etc., Petitioner,

v

RAYMOND H. HARVEY et al.

379 US 134, 13 L ed 2d 190, 85 S Ct 292

Argued October 20, 1964.
Decided December 7, 1964.

Decision: Suit to enjoin enforcement of union constitution and bylaws regarding eligibility for union office held beyond jurisdiction of federal court under § 102 of Labor-Management Reporting and Disclosure Act of 1959.

SUMMARY

Three union members brought suit in the United States District Court for the Southern District of New York to enjoin the union from preparing for or conducting any election until it revised its constitution and bylaws insofar as they deprived a union member of the right to nominate anyone for office but himself and provided that no member could be eligible for election to union office unless he had been a union member for five years and had served 180 days or more of sea time in each of two of the preceding three years on vessels covered by the union's collective bargaining agreements. The District Court dismissed the complaint for want of jurisdiction, reasoning that it did not allege a denial of the equal rights of union members to nominate candidates, guaranteed by § 101(a)(1) of the Labor-Management Reporting and Disclosure Act of 1959, and therefore was beyond the court's jurisdiction under § 102 of that statute. (221 F Supp 545.) The United States Court of Appeals for the Second Circuit reversed on the ground that the complaint alleged a violation of § 101(a)(1). (324 F2d 486.)

On certiorari, the Supreme Court of the United States reversed the judgment of the Court of Appeals and affirmed the judgment of the District Court. In an opinion by Black, J., expressing the views of six members of the Court, it was held that (1) the District Court's jurisdiction under § 102 depended entirely on whether the complaint alleged a violation of rights protected by Title I of the statute, such as the guaranty that union members and classes of members shall not be discriminated against in their right to nominate and vote, wholly apart from possible violations of provisions of Title IV of the statute, such as those dealing with eligibility for office, and (2) the complaint in the instant case "basically" related to eligibility for office, dealt with in Title IV rather than Title I of the statute.

Stewart, J., joined by Harlan, J., concurred on the ground that the complaint did not allege a violation of Title I rights, but also stated that a union's rules regarding nomination to office may be such as to violate Title I rights by curtailing the members' equal right to nominate within the meaning of Title I.

Douglas, J., expressed the view that he would affirm the Court of Appeals' judgment for the reasons stated in its opinion.

COUNSEL

David Scribner argued the cause for petitioner. With him on the brief was Lee Pressman.

Burton H. Hall argued the cause and filed a brief for respondents.

Briefs of amici curiae, urging reversal, were filed by Solicitor General Cox for the United States and by J. Albert Woll, Robert C. Mayer, Theodore J. St. Antoine and Thomas E. Harris for the American Federation of Labor and Congress of Industrial Organizations.

Briefs of amici curiae, urging affirmance, were filed by Melvin L. Wulf for the American Civil Liberties Union and by Rowland Watts for the Workers Defense League.

MABEL GILLESPIE, Administratrix, etc., Petitioner,

v

UNITED STATES STEEL CORPORATION

379 US 148, 13 L ed 2d 199, 85 S Ct 308

Argued October 13, 1964. Decided
December 7, 1964.

Decision: Jones Act held to preclude recovery, on ground
of unseaworthiness, for seaman's wrongful death in
territorial waters.

SUMMARY

Petitioner, the mother and administratrix of a seaman
who was drowned while working on a ship docked in
Ohio, sued the shipowner in the United States District
Court for the Northern District of Ohio, claiming a right
to recover for her own benefit and for the benefit of the
seaman's dependent brother and sisters under the Jones
Act for negligence, and under the Ohio wrongful death
statute for unseaworthiness. She also sought to recover
for the seaman's pain and suffering before he died, under
the Jones Act and general maritime law, which causes of
action the petitioner asserted survived the seaman's death
by virtue of the Jones Act and the Ohio survival statute.
The District Court, holding that the Jones Act supplied
the exclusive remedy, struck all parts of the complaint re-
ferring to the Ohio statutes or to unseaworthiness and also
struck all reference to recovery for the benefit of the seaman's brother and sisters. The Court of Appeals for the
Sixth Circuit affirmed. (321 F2d 518.)

On certiorari, the Supreme Court of the United States
affirmed except on the question whether the administratrix could recover for the seaman's pain and suffering
prior to death. In an opinion by **Black, J.**, expressing the
views of six members of the Court, it was held that (1)

the Court of Appeals did not err in holding that the trial court's order was "final" and therefore appealable under 28 USC § 1291, because the inconvenience and cost of the case would not be greater by deciding the appeal, a delay would result from refusing to decide the appeal, and the questions raised were fundamental to the further conduct of the case; (2) the Jones Act provides an exclusive right of action for the death of a seaman killed in the course of his employment by negligence, thus precluding recovery for unseaworthiness under the Ohio wrongful death statute; (3) the seaman's brother and sisters were not entitled to damages under the Jones Act, which limited recovery to the seaman's mother; and (4) the Jones Act did not preclude recovery for the seaman's pain and suffering prior to death, and the question whether recovery could be had under the Ohio survival statute for his pain and suffering was improperly decided on the pleading.

Harlan, J., dissented as to (1) on the ground that the trial court's order lacked finality.

Stewart, J., agreed with Mr. Justice Harlan that the trial court's order was not appealable, but on the merits he joined in the Court's opinion.

Goldberg, J., while agreeing with the majority as to (1), dissented as to (2) on the ground that an action should lie in federal court for a seaman's death within territorial waters as a result of unseaworthiness.

COUNSEL

Jack G. Day argued the cause for petitioner. With him on the brief was Bernard A. Berkman.

Thomas V. Koykka argued the cause for respondent. With him on the brief were McAlister Marshall and Robert B. Preston.

AMERICAN FEDERATION OF MUSICIANS, etc., et al., Petitioners,

v

EDDIE WITTSTEIN et al.

379 US 171, 13 L ed 2d 214, 85 S Ct 300

Argued November 16, 1964. Decided
December 7, 1964.

Decision: Weighted voting at union convention on proposal to increase dues held not violative of § 101 (a) (3)(B) of Labor-Management Reporting and Disclosure Act of 1959.

SUMMARY

Members of several American Federation of Musicians locals brought suit in the United States District Court for the Southern District of New York to annul a resolution increasing the per capita dues of all members, asserting that § 101(a)(3)(B) of the Labor-Management Reporting and Disclosure Act of 1959, providing that the dues of an international union shall not be increased except by majority vote of the delegates voting at a regular convention, prohibited the international from increasing its dues by the vote of delegates weighted and counted according to the number of members in the local which the delegate represented. The District Court entered summary judgment for the plaintiff union members (223 F Supp 27), and the United States Court of Appeals for the Second Circuit affirmed (326 F2d 26).

On certiorari, the Supreme Court of the United States reversed. In an opinion by **White, J.,** expressing the unanimous view of the seven participating members of the Court, it was held that § 101(a)(3)(B) does not prohibit a weighted voting system under which delegates cast a number of votes equal to the membership of the local union from which they are elected.

Warren, Ch. J., and **Goldberg,** J., did not participate.

COUNSEL

Henry Kaiser argued the cause for petitioners. With him on the brief were Eugene Gressman, George Kaufmann, David I. Ashe and Jerome H. Adler.

Godfrey P. Schmidt argued the cause and filed a brief for respondents.

Briefs of amici curiae, urging reversal, were filed by Solicitor General Cox for the United States, and by J. Albert Woll, Robert C. Mayer, Theodore J. St. Antoine and Thomas E. Harris for the American Federation of Labor and Congress of Industrial Organizations.

DEWEY McLAUGHLIN et al., Appellants,

v

STATE OF FLORIDA

379 US 184, 13 L ed 2d 222, 85 S Ct 283

Argued October 13 and 14, 1964. Decided
December 7, 1964.

Decision: Florida statute making it a criminal offense
for a white person and a Negro of opposite sexes to
habitually live in the same room held to violate equal
protection clause.

SUMMARY

Defendants were convicted in a Florida state court of
having violated a Florida statute which made it a criminal offense for a white person and a Negro of opposite
sexes, not married to each other, to habitually live in and
occupy in the nighttime the same room. The Florida
Supreme Court affirmed, and in reliance on Pace v Alabama, 106 US 583, 27 L ed 207, 1 S Ct 637, sustained the
validity of the statute as against the defendants' claims
that the statute denied them the equal protection of the
laws guaranteed by the Fourteenth Amendment. (153 So
2d 1.)

On appeal, the United States Supreme Court reversed.
In an opinion by **White, J.,** expressing the views of seven
members of the Court, it was held that, independently
of the validity of the Florida statute against interracial
marriages, the cohabitation statute under which the defendants were convicted was invalid as a denial of the
constitutional guaranty of equal protection of the laws.
It was pointed out that the narrow view of the equal protection clause taken in the Pace Case was swept away in
subsequent decisions of the Court.

Harlan, J., joined the Court's opinion in a separate concurring opinion.

Stewart, J., joined by Douglas, J., concurred, expressing the view that it is not possible for a state law to be valid which makes the criminality of an act depend on the race of the actor.

COUNSEL

William T. Coleman, Jr., and Louis H. Pollak argued the cause for appellants. With him on the briefs were Jack Greenberg and James M. Nabrit III.

James G. Mahorner, Assistant Attorney General of Florida, argued the cause for appellee. With him on the brief was James W. Kynes, Attorney General of Florida.

FIBREBOARD PAPER PRODUCTS CORPORA-
TION, Petitioner,

v

NATIONAL LABOR RELATIONS BOARD et al.

379 US 203, 13 L ed 2d 233, 85 S Ct 398

Argued October 19, 1964. Decided
December 14, 1964.

Decision: Employer which unilaterally decided to replace its maintenance employees by employees of independent contractor held to have violated its duty to bargain collectively with union representative of its employees.

SUMMARY

The National Labor Relations Board found that the respondent employer had violated § 8(a)(5) of the National Labor Relations Act by refusing to bargain collectively with the representative of its maintenance employees as regards the replacement of these employees by those of an independent contractor doing the same work. The Board ordered the employer to resume its maintenance operations, reinstate the employees with back pay, and bargain with the union. On appeal, the Court of Appeals for the District of Columbia Circuit granted the Board's petition for enforcement. (116 App DC 198, 322 F2d 411.)

On certiorari, the United States Supreme Court affirmed. In an opinion by Warren, Ch. J., expressing the views of five members of the Court, it was held that (1) the "contracting out" of work, as described above, was a subject of mandatory bargaining, and (2) the Board's order did not exceed its remedial powers.

Stewart, J., with the concurrence of Douglas and Harlan, JJ., concurred in the result, in an opinion which points out that, notwithstanding the broader language of the Court's opinion, its decision was limited to the question whether an employer may unilaterally decide to replace employees in a bargaining unit with those of an independent contractor or whether this is a subject of mandatory collective bargaining.

Goldberg, J., did not participate.

COUNSEL

Marion B. Plant argued the cause for petitioner. With him on the briefs was Gerard D. Reilly.

Solicitor General Cox argued the cause for respondent National Labor Relations Board. With him on the brief were Arnold Ordman, Dominick L. Manoli and Norton J. Come.

David E. Feller argued the cause for respondents United Steelworkers of America et al. With him on the brief were Elliot Bredhoff, Jerry D. Anker, Michael H. Gottesman and Jay Darwin.

Briefs of amici curiae, urging reversal, were filed by Eugene Adams Keeney and James W. Hunt for the Chamber of Commerce of the United States; Lambert H. Miller for the National Association of Manufacturers of the United States; and John B. Olverson for the Electronic Industries Association.

HOWARD FARMER, Petitioner,

v

ARABIAN AMERICAN OIL COMPANY (No. 32)

ARABIAN AMERICAN OIL COMPANY, Petitioner,

v

HOWARD FARMER (No. 33)

379 US 227, 13 L ed 2d 248, 85 S Ct 411

Argued November 9 and 10, 1964. Decided
December 14, 1964.

Decision: Prevailing party's expenses for transportation
of witnesses from Saudi Arabia to New York and for
daily transcripts of trial record held properly disallowed by District Court.

SUMMARY

An action for breach of an employment contract instituted by the employee in a New York state court was
removed to the United States District Court for the
Southern District of New York. District Judge Palmieri
granted the employer's motion for a directed verdict and
approved the clerk's taxation of costs against the employee, including the employer's transportation expenses for
witnesses brought from Saudi Arabia to New York and
costs for daily stenographic transcripts of the trial record
furnished to the employer's lawyers at their request. The
Court of Appeals for the Second Circuit reversed and remanded the case for a new trial. On a second trial before
District Judge Weinfeld, the jury found for the employer, and no appeal was taken. Accepting Judge Palmieri's
former cost taxation, the clerk then taxed $11,900.12

against the employee as the aggregate cost of both trials, but on review Judge Weinfeld reduced the costs to $831.60, lowering the cost bill approved by Judge Palmieri in the first trial from $6,601.08 to $496.05, chiefly by eliminating the transportation expenses of the witnesses and the expenses for the daily transcripts of the record. Judge Weinfeld also disallowed similar expenses in the second trial. (31 FRD 191.) Sitting en banc, the Court of Appeals, by a vote of five to four, affirmed Judge Weinfeld's cost taxation for the second trial, but reversed his cost taxation for the first trial, reducing, however, Judge Palmieri's cost allowance by $2,064 for transportation of two of the witnesses from Arabia occupying otherwise empty spaces in the employer's planes. (32 F2d 359.)

On writs of certiorari obtained by the employee and the employer, the United States Supreme Court reversed the judgment of the Court of Appeals and affirmed the judgment of the District Court. In an option by **Black, J.**, expressing the views of six of the members of the Court, it was held that (1) notwithstanding the rule that subpoenas requiring the attendance of witnesses at a trial cannot be served outside the judicial district more than 100 miles from the place of the trial, it is within the discretion of the trial court whether the transportation expenses for the witnesses should be allowed, (2) Judge Weinfeld was not bound by the former cost taxation of Judge Palmieri, and (3) the disallowance of both the transportation expenses and the expenses for the daily transcripts was within the proper exercise of Judge Weinfeld's discretion.

Goldberg, J., concurred in the result, expressing the view that the 100-mile rule is a limitation not to be departed from in taxing costs.

Harlan, J., joined by **Stewart, J.**, dissented on the ground that the scope of discretion of a district judge relied upon by the majority as basis of their decision is a matter which should be left with the courts of appeals.

COUNSEL

Kalman I. Nulman argued the cause for petitioner in No. 32 and respondent in No. 33. With him on the briefs was William V. Homans.

Chester Bordeau argued the cause for respondent in No. 32 and petitioner in No. 33. With him on the briefs were Lowell Wadmond, William L. Owen and Thomas F. Barry.

HEART OF ATLANTA MOTEL, Inc., Appellant,

v

UNITED STATES et al.

379 US 241, 13 L ed 2d 258, 85 S Ct 348

Argued October 5, 1964. Decided
December 14, 1964.

Decision: Sections 201(a)(b)(c)(e) and 203–207 of
Civil Rights Act of 1964 held constitutional as proper
exercise of commerce power.

SUMMARY

The corporate owner-operator of a motel which so-
licted and received patronage from interstate travelers
brought suit in the United States District Court for the
Northern District of Georgia for declaratory and injunctive relief preventing the Attorney General of the United
States from enforcing the public accommodations sections
of the Civil Rights Act of 1964 (78 Stat 241), as exceed-
ing the congressional power to regulate commerce, de-
priving it of liberty and property without due process of
law, taking its property without just compensation, and
subjecting it to involuntary servitude. The three-judge
District Court held the challenged provisions to be constitutional and enjoined the motel owner-operator from
discriminating against Negroes on account of race or
color. (231 F Supp 393.)

On direct appeal, the Supreme Court of the United
States affirmed. In an opinion by Clark, J., expressing
the views of eight members of the Court, it was held that
§§ 201(a)(b)(c)(e) and 203–207 of the Civil Rights Act
of 1964 are constitutional as a proper exercise of the
commerce power.

Black, J., concurring, stated that the statute as applied was valid under the commerce clause and the necessary and proper clause.

Douglas, J., concurring, joined in the Court's opinion but added that he preferred to base the constitutionality of the statute on the power conferred on Congress by § 5 of the Fourteenth Amendment.

Goldberg, J., concurring, joined in the Court's opinion but added that Congress had authority both under the commerce clause and § 5 of the Fourteenth Amendment to enact the statute.

COUNSEL

Moreton Rolleston, Jr., argued the cause and filed a brief for appellant.

Solicitor General Cox argued the cause for the United States et al. With him on the brief were Assistant Attorney General Marshall, Philip B. Heymann and Harold H. Greene.

Briefs of amici curiae, urging reversal, were filed by James W. Kynes, Attorney General of Florida, and Fred M. Burns and Joseph C. Jacobs, Assistant Attorneys General, for the State of Florida; and Robert Y. Button, Attorney General of Virginia, and Frederick T. Gray, Special Assistant Attorney General, for the Commonwealth of Virginia.

Briefs of amici curiae, urging affirmance, were filed by Thomas C. Lynch, Attorney Geeneral of California, Charles E. Corker and Dan Kaufmann, Assistant Attorneys General, and Charles B. McKesson and Jerold L. Perry, Deputy Attorneys General, for the State of California; Edward W. Brooke, Attorney General of Massachusetts, for the Commonwealth of Massachusetts; and

Louis J. Lefkowitz, Attorney General of New York, Samuel A. Hirshowitz, First Assistant Attorney General, and Shirley Adelson Siegel, Assistant Attorney General, for the State of New York.

NICHOLAS deB. KATZENBACH, Acting
Attorney General, et al., Appellants,

v

OLLIE McCLUNG, Sr., and Ollie McClung, Jr.

379 US 294, 13 L ed 2d 290, 85 S Ct 377

Argued October 5, 1964. Decided
December 14, 1964.

Decision: Section 201 (a) (b) (c) of Civil Rights Act of
1964 held constitutional as proper exercise of commerce power.

SUMMARY

The owner-operators of a Birmingham, Alabama, restaurant which discriminated against Negroes sued in the United States District Court for the Northern District of Alabama to enjoin the enforcement of Title II of the Civil Rights Act of 1964 (78 Stat 241) as unconstitutional. There was no claim that the restaurant's discrimination was supported by the state of Alabama or that interstate travelers frequented the restaurant, but it annually received about $70,000 worth of food which had moved in commerce. The three-judge District Court enjoined enforcement of the statute against the restaurant on the ground that the statute is unconstitutional. (233 F Supp 815.)

On direct appeal, the Supreme Court of the United States reversed. In an opinion by Clark, J., expressing the views of eight members of the Court, it was held that § 201 (a) (b) (c) of the statute, forbidding racial discrimination by restaurants offering to serve interstate travelers or serving food a substantial portion of which has moved in interstate commerce, is a constitutional exercise of the commerce power.

Black, J., concurring, stated that the statute as applied was valid under the commerce clause and the necessary and proper clause.

Douglas, J., concurring, joined in the Court's opinion but added that he preferred to base the constitutionality of the statute on the power conferred on Congress by § 5 of the Fourteenth Amendment.

Goldberg, J., concurring, joined in the Court's opinion but added that Congress had authority both under the commerce clause and § 5 of the Fourteenth Amendment to enact the statute.

COUNSEL

Solicitor General Cox argued the cause for appellants. With him on the brief were Assistant Attorney General Marshall, Ralph S. Spritzer, Philip B. Heymann, Harold H. Greene and Gerald P. Choppin.

Robert McDavid Smith argued the cause for appellees. With him on the briefs was William G. Somerville.

Jack Greenberg, Constance Baker Motley, James M. Nabrit III and Charles L. Black Jr., filed a brief for the NAACP Legal Defense and Educational Fund, Inc., as amicus curiae, urging reversal.

T. W. Bruton, Attorney General of North Carolina, and Ralph Moody, Deputy Attorney General, filed a brief for the State of North Carolina, as amicus curiae, urging affirmance.

ARTHUR HAMM, Jr., Petitioner,

v

CITY OF ROCK HILL (No. 2)

———

FRANK JAMES LUPPER et al., Petitioners,

v

STATE OF ARKANSAS (No. 5)

379 US 306, 13 L ed 2d 300, 85 S Ct 384

Argued October 12, 1964. Decided
December 14, 1964.

Decision: Civil Rights Act of 1964 held to abate state
trespass prosecutions of lunch counter sit-in demonstrators for conduct antedating enactment of statute.

SUMMARY

Before the enactment of the Civil Rights Act of 1964,
Negroes were convicted in the state courts of South Carolina and Arkansas of violating state trespass statutes by
participating in lunch counter sit-in demonstrations, and
their convictions were affirmed, respectively, by the Supreme Court of South Carolina (241 SC 420, 128 SE2d
907) and the Supreme Court of Arkansas (236 Ark 596,
367 SW2d 750).

On certiorari, the Supreme Court of the United States
vacated the judgments and ordered the charges dismissed.
In an opinion by **Clark, J.**, expressing the views of five
members of the Court, it was held that (1) the lunch
counters offered to serve interstate travelers, and were
places of public accommodation within the meaning of
the Civil Rights Act of 1964; (2) if the prosecutions were
federal prosecutions, they would have abated because of

that statute; and (3) the supremacy clause of the Federal Constitution required that the same rule be applied to state prosecutions, and since the state prosecutions were not finalized when the statute became law, they abated at that time.

Douglas, J., joined by Goldberg, J., joined in the Court's opinion but wrote a separate concurring opinion.

Black, J., dissented on the grounds that the Federal Saving Statute (1 USC § 109) prevented the courts from imputing to Congress an intent to abate cases retroactively, unless such an intent is expressly stated in the later statute, and that it was not the congressional intent in enacting the Civil Rights Act of 1964 to abate state prosecutions for conduct predating the enactment.

Harlan, J., dissented on the grounds that the abatement doctrine cannot be applied to the legislation of a different sovereignty, and Congress did not intend that the Civil Rights Act should displace past as well as prospective applications of state laws.

Stewart, J., dissented on the ground that Congress did not intend in passing the Civil Rights Act of 1964 that nonfinal state trespass convictions should abate.

White, J., dissented on the grounds that the Federal Saving Statute reversed the common-law presumption of abatement and Congress did not intend in enacting the Civil Rights Act of 1964 to void outstanding state court judgments.

COUNSEL

Jack Greenberg argued the cause for petitioner in No. 2. Constance Baker Motley argued the cause for petitioners in No. 5. With them on the brief were James M. Nabrit III, Charles L. Black Jr., Matthew J. Perry, Lincoln C.

Jenkins, Donald James Sampson, Willie T. Smith, Jr., Harold B. Anderson, Wiley A. Branton, William T. Coleman, Jr., and Marvin E. Frankel.

Daniel R. McLeod, Attorney General of South Carolina, argued the cause for respondent in No. 2. With him on the brief was Everett N. Brandon, Assistant Attorney General of South Carolina.

Jack L. Lessenberry, Chief Assistant Attorney General of Arkansas, argued the cause for respondent in No. 5. With him on the brief was Bruce Bennett, Attorney General of Arkansas.

ELIZABETH SIMONSON KING, etc.,
et al., Petitioners,

v

UNITED STATES

379 US 329, 13 L ed 2d 315, 85 S Ct 427

Argued October 19, 1964. Decided
December 14, 1964.

Decision: Distributing agent for corporate debtor in reorganization proceedings held personally liable for satisfying claims of nonpriority creditors, in consequence of which outstanding government priority claim could not be paid in full.

SUMMARY

The issue in the instant case was whether a distributing agent for a debtor corporation in a reorganization proceeding under Chapter XI of the Bankruptcy Act was personally liable to the government under 31 USC § 192 because he satisfied claims of nonpriority creditors with knowledge of an outstanding government priority claim, in consequence of which the government could not be paid in full. The issue arose in an action brought by the United States in the United States District Court for the District of New Jersey originally against such a distributing agent, and after his death continued against his executrix. The District Court dismissed the complaint on the theory that a distributing agent is not included within § 192, which makes liable to the government, in a situation as described above, an "executor, administrator, or assignee or other person." (208 F Supp 697.) On appeal, the Court of Appeals for the Third Circuit reversed. (322 F2d 317.)

On certiorari, the United States Supreme Court

affirmed the judgment of the Court of Appeals. In an opinion by **Harlan, J.**, expressing the views of six members of the Court, it was held that (1) whether or not the distributing agent falls within the category of fiduciaries described in § 192 depends upon the degree of control he is in a position to assert over the allocation among creditors of the debtor's assets in his possession, and (2) in the present case the distributing agent was in a sufficiently controlling position, on the grounds, among others, that as the president of the debtor corporation, he must have been aware of the government's potential claim, and that he was himself one of the major distributees.

White, J., concurred, on the ground that the facts in the present case justified holding the distributing agent liable to the government.

Black and **Douglas, JJ.**, dissented on the ground that § 192 did not cover a distributing agent for a corporate debtor in reorganization proceedings.

COUNSEL

David S. Bate argued the cause for petitioners. With him on the brief was Paul T. Murphy.

Alan S. Rosenthal argued the cause for the United States. With him on the brief were Solicitor General Cox, Assistant Attorney General Douglas, Hadley W. Libbey and Frederick B. Abramson.

ALL STATES FREIGHT, Inc., et al., Appellants,

v

NEW YORK, NEW HAVEN AND HARTFORD
RAILROAD COMPANY et al.

379 US 343, 13 L ed 2d 324, 85 S Ct 419

Argued October 21, 1964. Decided
December 14, 1964.

Decision: All-commodity railroad freight rates held not
subject to § 1(6) of Interstate Commerce Act.

SUMMARY

A railroad filed all-commodity rates with the Interstate
Commerce Commission, which disallowed them as violating § 1(6) of the Interstate Commerce Act, requiring
carriers to establish and observe just and reasonable classifications of property for transportation. (315 ICC 419.)
A three-judge United States District Court for the District of Connecticut set aside the Commission's order on
the ground that while § 1(6) requires the maintenance
of class rates, it does not apply to all-commodity rates.
(221 F Supp 370.)

On direct appeal, the Supreme Court of the United
States affirmed. In an opinion by **Stewart, J.**, expressing
the views of five members of the Court, it was held that
§ 1(6) empowers the Interstate Commerce Commission
to require that carriers maintain just and reasonable
classifications in conjunction with the setting of class
rates, but does not apply to all-commodity rates, which
are subject to regulation by the Commission under other
provisions of the statute.

White, J., joined by **Warren**, Ch. J., and **Black** and
Brennan, JJ., dissented on the ground that § 1(6) is not

inapplicable to a set of rates merely because it bears a commodity rate label.

COUNSEL

Homer S. Carpenter argued the cause for appellants. With him on the brief was John S. Fessenden.

Edward A. Kaier and Eugene E. Hunt argued the cause for appellees. With them on the brief were Margaret P. Allen and John A. Daily.

Robert W. Ginnane argued the cause for the United States and the Interstate Commerce Commission, urging reversal. With him on the brief were Solicitor General Cox, Assistant Attorney General Orrick, Frank Goodman, Lionel Kestenbaum and Fritz R. Kahn.

PARSONS et al.

v

BUCKLEY et al. (No. 624)

HOFF et al.

v

BUCKLEY et al. (No. 625)

379 US 359, 13 L ed 2d 352, 85 S Ct 503

January 12, 1965

Decision: Judgment in legislative apportionment case affirmed as modified in accordance with stipulation of parties permitting Federal District Court to reapportion state legislature.

SUMMARY

In a suit challenging the apportionment of the Vermont General Assembly, a three-judge United States District Court for the District of Vermont entered judgment which in paragraph (3) enjoined state and local officials from holding elections under the challenged apportionment system. (234 F Supp 191.)

On direct appeal to the Supreme Court of the United States, the court granted a motion by all the parties and intervenors to affirm the judgment below as modified by a stipulation deleting paragraph (3) and substituting therefor a paragraph which provided, among other things, that if reapportionment should not be effected by a certain date as a result of legislation or changes in the state constitution, the District Court should reapportion the General Assembly.

Harlan, J., stated in a separate memorandum that without plenary and deliberate consideration by the Court, he would not approve that part of the stipulation which authorized the District Court to reapportion the legislature.

COUNSEL

George D. Webster for appellants in No. 624. Charles E. Gibson, Jr., Attorney General of Vermont, and Chester S. Ketcham, Deputy Attorney General, for appellants in No. 625.

Joseph A. McNamara for appellees.

PEOPLE OF THE STATE OF CALIFORNIA
et al., Petitioners,

v

LO-VACA GATHERING COMPANY et al.
(No. 46)

SOUTHERN CALIFORNIA GAS COMPANY
et al., Petitioners,

v

LO-VACA GATHERING COMPANY et al.
(No. 47)

FEDERAL POWER COMMISSION, Petitioner,

v

LO-VACA GATHERING COMPANY et al.
(No. 57)

379 US 366, 13 L ed 2d 357, 85 S Ct 486

Argued November 17 and 18, 1964. Decided
January 18, 1965.

Decision: Natural gas sales held within Federal Power
Commission's jurisdiction where gas was contractually restricted to use solely as fuel in pipeline company's facilities but a substantial part of it was in
fact resold in interstate commerce as a result of commingling with other gas.

SUMMARY

In a proceeding before the Federal Power Commission,
the Commission entered an order declaring to be within
its jurisdiction, as sales of natural gas in interstate com-

merce "for resale," sales of natural gas in Texas, produced and delivered there, but flowing in a commingled stream with gas from other sources, and at least a portion of which would be resold out of Texas, notwithstanding the fact that the gas was sold to a pipeline company under a "restricted use" agreement providing that the gas delivered in Texas would be metered, that all of it would be used solely as fuel in the buyer's facilities outside of Texas, and that the buyer would meter the gas used by it for fuel purposes in such facilities to make certain that such amount invariably exceeded the volume of gas purchased under the agreement. The United States Court of Appeals for the Fifth Circuit reversed. (323 F2d 190.)

On certiorari, the Supreme Court of the United States reversed. In an opinion by **Douglas, J.**, expressing the views of seven members of the Court, it was held that (1) the fact that a substantial part of the gas would be resold invoked federal jurisdiction at the outset over the entire transaction, and (2) the line between "jurisdictional" and "non-jurisdictional" sales could be drawn by the Commission on a case-by-case basis through the use of its adjudicatory power, without the exercise of its rule-making power.

Harlan, J., dissented on the ground that the case should be remanded to the Commission for further proceedings after the promulgation by the Commission of interpretive rules to cover it and like cases.

White, J., did not participate.

COUNSEL

Richard E. Tuttle argued the cause for petitioners in No. 46. With him on the briefs were J. Calvin Simpson and John T. Murphy.

John Ormasa argued the cause for petitioners in No. 47. With him on the brief was Milford Springer.

Richard A. Solomon argued the cause for petitioner in No. 57. With him on the brief were Solicitor General Cox, Ralph S. Spritzer, Frank I. Goodman, Howard E. Wahrenbrock, Robert L. Russell and Peter H. Schiff.

Sherman S. Poland argued the cause for respondents. With him on the brief were Bradford Ross, C. Frank Reifsnyder and Hugh Q. Buck.

Harry L. Albrecht filed a brief for the Independent Natural Gas Association of America, as amicus curiae, urging affirmance.

———————

UNITED STATES, Petitioner,

v

FIRST NATIONAL CITY BANK

379 US 378, 13 L ed 2d 365, 85 S Ct 528

Argued November 16, 1964. Decided
January 18, 1965.

Decision: Temporary injunction issued by Federal District Court against national bank in New York with branch office in Uruguay, freezing property of Uruguay corporation under 26 USC § 7402(a), held the reasonable measure to protect jeopardy tax assessments.

SUMMARY

To protect its jeopardy income tax assessments against a Uruguayan corporation, the government obtained, in the United States District Court for the Southern District of New York, a temporary injunction against a national bank located in New York City, with a branch office in Uruguay, enjoining the bank from transferring any property or rights to property of the taxpayer held by the bank or by any of its branch offices within or without the United States, the District Court indicating that it would modify the order should compliance be shown to violate the law of Uruguay. (210 F Supp 773.) The Court of Appeals for the Second Circuit reversed by a divided vote both by a panel of three judges (321 F2d 14) and en banc (325 F2d 1020). At the time of the issuance of the injunction the taxpayer was beyond the reach of the District Court insofar as personal service was concerned, but a subsequently enacted New York statute made out-of-state service possible. However, no such service had been made at the date of argument of the case in the United States Supreme Court.

On certiorari, the Supreme Court reversed the judgment of the Court of Appeals. In an opinion by Douglas, J., expressing the views of seven members of the Court, the injunction was held a reasonable measure to protect the status quo and within the jurisdiction conferred upon the District Court by 26 USC § 7402(a), giving District Courts power to grant injunctions "necessary or appropriate for the enforcement of the Internal Revenue Laws."

Harlan, J., joined by Goldberg, J., dissented, expressing the view that the course taken by the majority could not be sustained without extending federal court jurisdiction beyond permissible limits.

COUNSEL

Assistant Attorney General Oberdorfer argued the cause for the United States. With him on the briefs were Solicitor General Cox and Harold C. Wilkenfeld.

Henry Harfield argued the cause for respondent. With him on the brief were William Harvey Reeves and John E. Hoffman, Jr.

Roy C. Haberkern, Jr., and Edward J. Ross filed a brief for the Chase Manhattan Bank et al., as amici curiae, urging affirmance.

Theodore Tannenwald and A. Chauncey Newlin filed a memorandum for Omar, S. A.

WHITNEY NATIONAL BANK IN JEFFERSON PARISH, Petitioner,

v

BANK OF NEW ORLEANS AND TRUST COMPANY et al. (No. 26)

JAMES J. SAXON, Comptroller of the Currency, Petitioner,

v

BANK OF NEW ORLEANS AND TRUST COMPANY et al. (No. 30)

379 US 411, 13 L ed 2d 386, 85 S Ct 551

Argued November 12, 1964. Decided January 18, 1965.

Decision: Federal Reserve Board, and not Federal District Court, held to have jurisdiction to determine controversy between state-chartered banks and national bank as to plan to create new national banks operated by bank holding company.

SUMMARY

    The present controversy arose between a national bank and three state-chartered banking competitors. To avoid the restrictions of the federal banking laws as to branch banking, a national bank operating in a parish of Louisiana resorted to a plan under which a holding company would organize a new national bank, the existing bank would merge into that bank, and the holding company would also organize another new national bank to operate in an adjoining parish. After approval of the plan by the Federal Reserve Board and several days after the Board's denial of a petition for reconsideration, Louisiana enacted a statute making it unlawful for a bank holding company to open for business any bank not presently open for business. The state-chartered banks sought judicial review of the Federal Reserve Board decision in the Court of Appeals for the Fifth Circuit. This suit is presently pending in that court.

Meanwhile, the state-chartered banks commenced the present suit in the United States District Court for the District of Columbia, seeking a declaratory judgment and injunctive relief against the Comptroller of the Currency to prevent him from issuing the requisite certificate of authority for the new bank. A permanent injunction was issued (211 F Supp 576) and upheld by the Court of Appeals for the District of Columbia Circuit (116 App DC 285, 323 F2d 290).

On writs of certiorari, the United States Supreme Court reversed the judgment of the Court of Appeals and remanded the case to the District Court with direction to dismiss the complaint. The mandate was stayed for 60 days to afford the parties, which included the existing federal bank, opportunity to move in the Court of Appeals for the Fifth Circuit for an order remanding the case pending there to the Federal Reserve Board, and to permit that Court of Appeals to issue orders against the issuance of a certificate by the Comptroller. In an opinion by Clark, J., expressing the views of seven members of the Court, it was held that the District Court of the District of Columbia had no jurisdiction to pass on the merits of the holding company proposal and that appropriate disposition of the controversy could not be made without further consideration of the effect of the Louisiana statute by the Federal Reserve Board, where original exclusive jurisdiction rests.

Douglas, J., dissented (1) from the Court's rulings that the District Court had no jurisdiction of the controversy with the Comptroller; and (2) from remitting the question of constitutionality of the Louisiana statute to the Federal Reserve Board. He would decide the latter issue in the present proceeding.

Black, J., also dissenting, agreed with the dissenting opinion of Douglas, J., but would go further and affirm the District Court's judgment.

COUNSEL

Dean Acheson argued the cause for petitioner in No. 26. With him on the briefs were Malcolm L. Monroe, Brice M. Clagett and Walter J. Suthon III.

Ralph S. Spritzer argued the cause for petitioner in No. 30. On the brief were Solicitor General Cox, Philip B. Heymann, Morton Hollander and David L. Rose.

Edward L. Merrigan argued the cause for respondents. With him on the brief for respondent banks were A. J. Waechter, Jr., James W. Bean and Charles W. Lane. With him on the brief for respondent Louisiana State Bank Commissioner was Joseph H. Kavanaugh, Assistant Attorney General of Louisiana.

Briefs of amici curiae, urging affirmance, were filed by James F. Bell for the National Association of Supervisors of State Banks, and by Horace R. Hansen for the Independent Bankers Association.

BEN W. FORTSON, Jr., Secretary of State of
the State of Georgia, Appellant,

v

JAMES W. DORSEY et al.

379 US 433, 13 L ed 2d 401, 85 S Ct 498

Argued December 10, 1964. Decided
January 18, 1965.

Decision: Georgia statute providing for countywide election of multimember state senatorial delegations held
not unconstitutional on its face.

SUMMARY

Registered voters in Georgia brought suit before a
three-judge United States District Court for the Northern
District of Georgia for declaratory and injunctive relief
against a Georgia statute which apportioned the state's
54 senatorial seats among 54 senatorial districts drawn,
as far as possible, along existing county lines, and with
no mathematical disparity, but provided that where there
was more than one district in a county, all the county's
senators should be elected by a countywide vote. The
court held that the statute was null and void as violative
of the equal protection clause of the Fourteenth Amendment. (228 F Supp 259.)

On direct appeal, the Supreme Court of the United
States reversed. In an opinion by **Brennan, J.**, expressing
the views of eight members of the Court, it was held that
absent any contention that there was not substantial
equality of population among the districts, or evidence to
support the assertion that the scheme was intended to
minimize or cancel out the voting strength of racial or
political elements of the voting population, the statute
was constitutional.

Harlan, J., concurring, joined in the Court's opinion and judgment with the reservation that its opinion should not be taken to mean that the constitutionality of state legislative apportionments must always be judged in terms of simple arithmetic.

Douglas, J., dissented on the ground that the statute constituted an invidious discrimination violating the Fourteenth Amendment.

COUNSEL

Paul Rodgers, Assistant Attorney General of Georgia, argued the cause for appellant. With him on the brief was Eugene Cook, Attorney General of Georgia.

Edwin F. Hunt argued the cause for appellees. With him on the brief were William C. O'Kelley and Charles A. Moye, Jr.

AARON HENRY, Petitioner,

v

STATE OF MISSISSIPPI

379 US 443, 13 L ed 2d 408, 85 S Ct 564

Argued October 13, 1964. Decided
January 18, 1965.

Decision: Mississippi state judgment affirming conviction
based on illegally obtained evidence, to which no
contemporaneous objection was made, vacated and
case remanded for hearing on question whether accused waived decision of federal claim.

SUMMARY

During his trial in the County Court of Bolivar County,
Mississippi, on a charge of disturbing the peace, the accused's counsel failed to object to the admission of a
police officer's testimony regarding what he found during
an unlawful search of the accused's automobile, but at
the close of the state's evidence his counsel asked for a
directed verdict because of the erroneous admission of
the officer's testimony. The motion was denied, the accused was convicted, and the conviction was upheld by
the Supreme Court of Mississippi on the grounds that
the counsel's "honest mistakes" were binding on the accused and that the counsel's cross-examination of the
officer before the motion for a directed verdict and his
introduction of other evidence of the car's interior afterward "cured" the original error and estopped the accused
to complain of the tainted evidence. (154 So 2d 289.)

On certiorari, the Supreme Court of the United States
vacated the judgment below and remanded for a rehearing on the question whether the accused was to be deemed
to have knowingly waived decision of his federal claim

when timely objection was not made to the admission of the illegally seized evidence. In an opinion by **Brennan, J.**, expressing the views of five members of the Court, it was held that (1) a litigant's procedural defaults in state proceedings do not prevent vindication of his federal rights unless the state's insistence on compliance with its procedural rule serves a legitimate state interest; (2) the Mississippi rule requiring contemporaneous objection to the introduction of illegal evidence serves a legitimate state interest, but the purpose of the rule may have been substantially served by the motion for a directed verdict; (3) if such were the case, the conviction would not rest on an adequate state ground so as to preclude review of the claim by the Supreme Court; (4) even if the motion for a directed verdict satisfied the state interest served by the contemporaneous objection rule, the record suggested a possibility that the accused's counsel forfeited his state court remedies by deliberately bypassing the opportunity to make a timely objection in the state court, as a part of trial strategy, thereby precluding the accused from asserting his constitutional claim; and (5) the state should have an opportunity to establish the fact of waiver.

Black, J., dissenting, stated that (1) he would not remand for a hearing on the issue of waiver, because the record was barren of evidence to support a finding that there was a waiver, and because if there was a real issue as to waiver, it should be decided by the Supreme Court itself; and (2) the Mississippi contemporaneous-objection rule was not an adequate state ground precluding the Supreme Court's review of the constitutional issue, because the Mississippi Supreme Court has power to consider constitutional questions, regardless of when they are presented.

Harlan, J., joined by **Clark** and **Stewart, JJ.**, dissenting, stated that the writ of certiorari should be dismissed as improvidently granted, since the Mississippi contemporaneous-objection rule was an adequate state ground so as to preclude Supreme Court review of the constitutional issue.

COUNSEL

Barbara A. Morris argued the cause for petitioner. With her on the brief were Robert L. Carter, Jack H. Young, R. Jess Brown, Jr., and Alvin K. Hellerstein.

G. Garland Lyell, Jr., Assistant Attorney General of Mississippi, argued the cause for respondent. With him on the brief was Joe T. Patterson, Attorney General of Mississippi.

WAYNE TURNER, Petitioner,

v

STATE OF LOUISIANA

379 US 466, 13 L ed 2d 424, 85 S Ct 546

Argued November 19, 1964. Decided
January 18, 1965.

Decision: Due process guaranty of Fourteenth Amendment held violated by association, during murder trial, of jurors and deputy sheriffs who were key prosecution witnesses.

SUMMARY

During a three-day murder prosecution in the Twenty-First Judicial District Court, Parish of Tangipahoa, Louisiana, two deputy sheriffs who were the two principal prosecution witnesses were in continuous and intimate association with the jurors, eating with them, conversing with them, and doing errands for them. The accused's counsel moved for a mistrial when the deputies testified, and moved for a new trial after the jury returned a guilty verdict. The motions were denied and the accused was sentenced to death. The Supreme Court of Louisiana affirmed on the ground that there was no showing of prejudice. (244 La 447, 152 So 2d 555.)

On certiorari, the Supreme Court of the United States reversed. In an opinion by Stewart, J., expressing the views of eight members of the Court, it was held that the conduct of the trial violated the basic guaranties of trial by jury, in violation of the Fourteenth Amendment, since the credibility which the jury attached to the deputies' testimony must inevitably have determined whether the accused would be convicted.

Clark, J., dissented on the ground that since no prejudice was shown, the practice did not reach federal due process proportions.

COUNSEL

Allen B. Pierson, Jr., argued the cause for petitioner. With him on the brief was Burrell J. Carter.

Leonard E. Yokum argued the cause for respondent. With him on the brief were Jack P. F. Gremillion, Attorney General of Louisiana, M. E. Culligan, Assistant Attorney General, and Duncan S. Kemp.

JOHN W. STANFORD, Jr., Petitioner,

v

STATE OF TEXAS

379 US 476, 13 L ed 2d 431, 85 S Ct 506

Argued November 12, 1964. Decided
January 18, 1965.

Decision: Search warrant authorizing the seizure of all
literary material concerning the Communist Party
of Texas and its operations held invalid under Fourth
Amendment.

SUMMARY

A search warrant issued by a Texas county judge authorized the seizure of all kinds of literary material and
documents concerning the Communist Party of Texas
and its operations. On the strength of this warrant several Texas law-enforcement officers seized some 2,000
of the petitioner's books, pamphlets, and papers. As
against his contention that the search and seizure violated the Fourth Amendment, the magistrate denied petitioner's motion to annul the warrant and order the return
of the property seized. This order of denial was final
and not appealable or otherwise reviewable under Texas
law.

On certiorari to the Fifty-Seventh Judicial District
Court of Bexar County, Texas, the United States Supreme
Court vacated the order of the county judge. In an
opinion by **Stewart, J.,** expressing the unanimous view of
the Court, it was held that the indiscriminate sweep of
the language of the search warrant was constitutionally
intolerable.

COUNSEL

Maury Maverick, Jr., and John J. McAvoy argued the cause for petitioner. With them on the briefs was Melvin L. Wulf.

James E. Barlow and Hawthorne Phillips argued the cause for respondent. With them on the brief were Waggoner Carr, Attorney General of Texas, and Howard M. Fender and Lonny F. Zwiener, Assistant Attorneys General.

NICK JANKOVICH and Paul Jankovich,
Co-Partners, doing business as Calumet
Aviation Company, Petitioners,

v

INDIANA TOLL ROAD COMMISSION

379 US 487, 13 L ed 2d 439, 85 S Ct 493

Argued December 10, 1964. Decided
January 18, 1965.

Decision: Judgment invalidating, because taking plaintiff's property for public use without compensation, city zoning ordinance prescribing height limitations with regard to structures near municipal airport, held to rest on adequate state ground and hence not reviewable by United States Supreme Court.

SUMMARY

The lessees and operators of the municipal airport of the city of Gary, Indiana, instituted the present action in an Indiana state court against the Indiana Toll Road Commission for injunctive relief and damages, contending that defendant constructed a toll road parallel to the south side of the airport and thereby violated the height limitations of a city ordinance concerning buildings and other structures in the vicinity of the airport. While denying injunctive relief, the trial court awarded plaintiffs damages of $164,000. The Supreme Court of Indiana reversed, holding the ordinance invalid because purporting to authorize an unlawful and unconstitutional appropriation of property rights without payment of compensation. (193 NE2d 237.)

A writ of certiorari granted to plaintiffs was dismissed by the United States Supreme Court as improvidently granted. In an opinion by **White, J.,** expressing the views of seven members of the Court, it was held that the United States Supreme Court had no jurisdiction to review the state judgment because it was rested on an adequate state ground. It was pointed out that while the Indiana Supreme Court considered both the pertinent provisions of the Indiana Constitution and the Fourteenth Amendment to the Federal Constitution, nothing in the state court's opinion suggested that its conclusion flowed from a federal rather than a state source or was placed less forcefully on the state constitution than on the Fourteenth Amendment.

Stewart, J., joined by Black, J., dissented. Finding no clear indication in the opinion of the court below as to whether that court's conclusion was based upon the Federal Constitution, the state constitution, or both, they would vacate the judgment and remand the cause to the Indiana Supreme Court for clarification of its opinion.

COUNSEL

Bernard Dunau argued the cause for petitioners. With him on the briefs were Straley Thorpe, Robert C. Lester and Rita C. Davidson.

Hugh B. Cox argued the cause for respondent. With him on the brief were Charles A. Miller, Paul J. DeVault and Philip E. Byron, Jr.

Briefs of amici curiae, urging reversal, were filed by Solicitor General Cox and Roger P. Marquis for the United States; by Edwin K. Steers, Attorney General of Indiana, Harold L. Folley, Deputy Attorney General, and John J. Dillon for the Aeronautics Commission of Indiana et al.; by Roger Arnebergh, Alexander G. Brown, J. Elliott Drinard, Sidney Goldstein, Daniel B. Goldberg, Henry P. Kucera, John C. Melaniphy, Robert E. Michalski, Thomas J. Neenan, John W. Sholenberger, Barnett

I. Shur, Fred G. Stickel III, Charles S. Rhyne, Brice W. Rhyne and Alfred J. Tighe, Jr., for the National Institute of Municipal Law Officers; and by John E. Stephen and George S. Laphan, Jr., for the Air Transport Association.

CITY OF EL PASO, Appellant,

v

GREENBERRY SIMMONS

379 US 497, 13 L ed 2d 446, 85 S Ct 577

Argued November 17, 1964. Decided
January 18, 1965.

Decision: Constitutional prohibition against impairing
obligation of contracts held not violated by application to previous land sales of Texas statute requiring
exercise, within five years after forfeiture of lands
for nonpayment of interest, of right to reinstatement
from forfeiture.

SUMMARY

In a trespass to try title suit brought in the United
States District Court for the Western District of Texas,
it was shown that the land in question was sold by the
state in 1910 under a statute providing for the forfeiture
of the land to the state in the event of nonpayment of
interest under the contract of sale, and also providing
that in case of forfeiture the purchaser or his vendee could
reinstate his claim by paying the full amount of interest
due.   The statute was amended in 1941 to provide that
the right of reinstatement "must be exercised within five
years from the date of forfeiture."   The land in question
was forfeited on July 21, 1947.   The plaintiff thereafter
took quitclaim deeds to it and on July 23, 1952, he filed
applications for reinstatement, with checks for the un-
paid interest.   The applications were denied as untimely,
and the state later sold the land to a municipality, against
whom the plaintiff brought suit.   The District Court
entered summary judgment for the city, but the United

States Court of Appeals for the Fifth Circuit reversed on the ground that the constitutional prohibition against impairment of contracts forbade application of the 1941 statute to the contract in question. (320 F2d 541.)

On appeal, the Supreme Court of the United States reversed. In an opinion by **White, J.**, expressing the views of eight members of the Court, it was held that not every modification of a contractual promise impairs the obligation of contract, and that in view of the 1941 statute's purpose of restoring the stability and integrity of land titles and enabling the state to protect and administer its property in a businesslike manner, it did not impair a right protected under the contract clause.

Black, J., dissenting, expressed the view that the majority was "balancing away" constitutional rights in order to save the state from "a bad bargain."

COUNSEL

William J. Mounce argued the cause for appellant. With him on the brief was Thornton Hardie.

Greenberry Simmons, appellee, argued the cause and filed a brief pro se.

B. ELTON COX, Appellant,

v

STATE OF LOUISIANA

379 US 536, 13 L ed 2d 471, 85 S Ct 453

Argued October 12, 1964. Decided
January 18, 1965.

Decision: Conviction of civil rights leader for breach of
the peace and obstructing public passages held unconstitutional as abridging freedom of speech and
assembly.

SUMMARY

After a trial in the Nineteenth Judicial District for
the Parish of East Baton Rouge, Louisiana, a civil rights
leader was convicted of breach of the peace, obstructing
public passages, and picketing before a courthouse.† The
charges were based on his conduct during a demonstration of 2,000 Negro college students protesting racial
discrimination and the arrest of 23 fellow students, during which they assembled peaceably at the state capitol
building, marched to the courthouse where the 23 fellow
students were locked in jail cells, and with official permission assembled again on the sidewalk across the street
and 101 feet from the courthouse steps, and in an orderly
manner, sang, prayed, and listened to the leader's speech,
but failed to disperse on police order that they had exceeded their time for demonstrating. The Supreme Court
of Louisiana affirmed the convictions. (244 La 1087,
156 So 2d 448; 245 La 303, 158 So 2d 172.)

On appeal from the affirmance of the convictions of
disturbing the peace and obstructing public passages,
the Supreme Court of the United States reversed. In

---

† The majority opinion on the conviction of picketing before
a courthouse is summarized on p. 71, infra.

an opinion by **Goldberg, J.**, expressing the views of five members of the Court, it was held that (1) the breach of the peace conviction infringed the leader's rights of free speech and assembly because (a) he did not engage in any conduct which the state had a right to prohibit as a breach of the peace and (b) the breach of the peace statute, as construed by the state courts' definition of breach of the peace as to agitate or to disquiet, was unconstitutionally broad in scope in that it would allow punishment merely for peacefully expressing unpopular views; and (2) the conviction for unlawfully obstructing public passages was an unwarranted abridgment of the leader's freedom of speech and assembly because the city authorities permitted or prohibited parades or street meetings in their completely uncontrolled discretion.

Black, J., concurred on the grounds that (1) the breach of the peace statute on its face and as construed by the state courts was so broad as to be unconstitutionally vague, and (2) since the obstructing public passages statute specifically permitted picketing for the publication of labor union views, it constituted both censorship forbidden by the First and Fourteenth Amendments and an invidious discrimination forbidden by the equal protection clause of the Fourteenth Amendment.

Clark, J., concurred on the grounds that while the breach of the peace statute was not unconstitutionally vague, both this statute and the obstructing public passages statute were unconstitutional under the equal protection clause since they expressly excluded labor union activities.

White, J., joined by **Harlan, J.**, (1) concurred in the reversal of the breach of the peace conviction because the leader could not be punished for expressing unpopular views, but (2) dissented from the reversal of the conviction of obstructing public passages, stating that the statute had not been applied as an "open-ended licensing statute."

COUNSEL

Carl Rachlin argued the cause for appellant. With him on the brief were Robert Collins, Nils Douglas and Floyd McKissick.

Ralph L. Roy argued the cause for appellee. With him on the brief was Jack P. F. Gremillion, Attorney General of Louisiana.

B. ELTON COX, Appellant,

v

STATE OF LOUISIANA

379 US 559, 13 L ed 2d 487, 85 S Ct 476

Argued October 21 and 22, 1964. Decided
January 18, 1965.

Decision: State conviction of picketing near courthouse
held violative of due process where officials gave permission for picketing.

SUMMARY

A civil rights leader was convicted in the Nineteenth
Judicial District for the Parish of East Baton Rouge,
Louisiana, of picketing near a courthouse, based on the
same set of facts as those in Cox v Louisiana, supra, p. 68.
The Supreme Court of Louisiana affirmed. (245 La 303,
158 So 2d 172.)

On appeal, the Supreme Court of the United States
reversed. In an opinion by Goldberg, J., expressing the
views of five members of the Court, it was held that
the conviction violated due process of law as "an in-
defensible sort of entrapment" because city officials in
effect told the demonstrators that they could meet where
they did.

Black, J., joined by Harlan and White, JJ., dissented on
the ground that officials cannot authorize violations of
criminal laws, testimony in the record denied that the
permission was given, and even if given it was soon
afterward revoked.

Clark, J., dissented on the ground that no permission
was given for the picketing, and even if given, it was
not binding on the state.

COUNSEL

Nils Douglas argued the cause for appellant. With him on the brief were Carl Rachlin, Robert Collins and Floyd McKissick.

Ralph L. Roy argued the cause for appellee. With him on the brief was Jack P. F. Gremillion, Attorney General of Louisiana.

SECURITIES AND EXCHANGE
COMMISSION, Petitioner,

v

AMERICAN TRAILER RENTALS CO.

379 US 594, 13 L ed 2d 510, 85 S Ct 513

Argued November 10, 1964. Decided
January 18, 1965.

Decision: Reorganization proceeding under Chapter X
of Bankruptcy Act, rather than composition proceeding under Chapter XI, held necessary where
rights of widespread public investor-creditors were
materially affected.

SUMMARY

After a company engaged in the business of renting
automobile trailers had petitioned for a composition of
creditors under Chapter XI of the Bankruptcy Act, the
Securities and Exchange Commission filed a motion to
dismiss the company's proceeding or, in effect, to transfer
it to Chapter X of the Bankruptcy Act, involving corporate reorganization proceedings. The Commission's
motion, based on the need for protecting the rights of
widespread public investor-creditors of the company, was
referred to a referee in bankruptcy as a special master,
and the referee recommended that the motion be denied.
The District Court, accepting and adopting the referee's
findings, denied the motion, and the United States Court
of Appeals for the Tenth Circuit affirmed (325 F2d 47).

On certiorari, the Supreme Court of the United States
reversed and held that the Commission's motion should
have been granted. In an opinion by **Goldberg, J.,** expressing the unanimous view of the Court, it was decided
that all issues relevant to the company's possible financial

rehabilitation had to be determined in a Chapter X proceeding, which would provide greater protection of public investors' interests than would a Chapter XI proceeding.

COUNSEL

Daniel M. Friedman argued the cause for petitioner. With him on the briefs were Solicitor General Cox, Philip A. Loomis, Jr., and David Ferber.

Arthur W. Burke, Jr., argued the cause and filed a brief for respondent.

Marcien Jenckes argued the cause and filed a brief for the State Mutual Life Assurance Company of America et al., as amici curiae.

BEN W. FORTSON, Jr., as Secretary of the
State of Georgia, et al., Appellants,

v

HENRY J. TOOMBS et al.

379 US 621, 13 L ed 2d 527, 85 S Ct 598

Argued November 18 and 19, 1964. Decided
January 18, 1965.

Decision: Federal court order enjoining the proposal of
a new state constitution by a malapportioned state
legislature vacated and remanded for reconsideration of its desirability and need in view of election
of new legislature and speculative nature of question
of what it might do.

SUMMARY

In a suit challenging the validity of the apportionment
of the Georgia legislature, a three-judge United States
District Court for the Northern District of Georgia entered a decree (1) declaring the legislative apportionment
invalid after the November, 1964, general election; (2)
enjoining state election officials from placing on the ballot,
until the legislature was reapportioned in accordance with
constitutional standards, the question whether a constitutional amendment should be adopted amending the state
constitution by substituting an entirely new constitution
therefor; and (3) limiting the service of the 1965 state
house of representatives to such business as should properly come before it during the regular 45-day session.
After the appeal was argued in the Supreme Court of
the United States, the District Court struck paragraph
(3) and substituted therefor a paragraph limiting the
service of the 1965 house of representatives to one year's
duration.

On direct appeal to the Supreme Court of the United States, paragraph (2) was vacated in a per curiam order, expressing the views of six members of the Court, remanding the case to the District Court for reconsideration of its desirability and need in light of the results of the 1964 election, in which new members were elected to both houses of the state legislature, and the appellees' suggestion that it was highly speculative as to what the 1965 legislature might do.

Clark, J., concurring, stated that he would prefer to declare the litigation moot and vacate the judgment below, but that he joined in the court's opinion and judgment solely on the ground that it was not deciding the propriety of the decree.

Harlan, J., joined by Stewart, J., concurring in part and dissenting in part, stated that neither paragraph (2) nor original paragraph (3) was moot, and that since both of such paragraphs were improvident, the decree should be modified by striking paragraph (2) and approving the substitution for the original paragraph (3).

Goldberg, J., dissenting, stated that the case was moot, and that the proper disposition of it was to vacate paragraph (2) and dismiss the appeal.

COUNSEL

E. Freeman Leverett, Deputy Assistant Attorney General of Georgia, argued the cause for appellants. With him on the brief was Eugene Cook, Attorney General of Georgia.

Francis Shackelford argued the cause for appellees. With him on the brief were Emmet J. Bondurant II, J. Quentin Davidson, Edward S. White and Hamilton Lokey.

REPUBLIC STEEL CORPORATION, Petitioner,

v

CHARLIE MADDOX

379 US 650, 13 L ed 2d 580, 85 S Ct 614

Argued November 18, 1964. Decided
January 25, 1965.

Decision: Federal labor policy requiring exhaustion of
grievance procedures held applicable so as to bar
employee's state court action against interstate employer for severance pay allegedly due under terms of
collective bargaining agreement.

SUMMARY

An employee sued his employer in an Alabama state
court for severance pay which was allegedly due under
the terms of a collective bargaining agreement between
the employer and the employee's union. The employer
was engaged in interstate commerce, and its industrial relations were subject to the provisions of the Labor Management Relations Act. Nearly 3 years prior to the
commencement of the action, the employee had been
laid off. The collective bargaining agreement authorized
severance pay if the layoff resulted from the employer's
decision to close its mine permanently, but the agreement
also provided for a three-step grievance procedure, to be
followed by binding arbitration. The case was tried
on stipulated facts without a jury, and although the
employee had made no effort to utilize the grievance
procedures which were provided by the collective bargaining agreement, judgment was awarded in his favor
for the amount which he claimed was due him. The
Alabama Court of Appeals and the Alabama Supreme
Court (275 Ala 685, 158 So 2d 492) affirmed on the

grounds that state law was applicable to a suit for severance pay and that, under Alabama law, an employee was not required to exhaust his grievance procedures as a prerequisite to bringing such a suit.

On certiorari, the United States Supreme Court reversed. In an opinion by Harlan, J., expressing the views of eight members of the Court, it was held that federal law, rather than state law, applied, and that, in accordance with the policies embodied in the Labor Management Relations Act, the employee's failure to utilize the grievance procedures provided by the collective bargaining agreement precluded him from being able to sue his employer for severance pay.

Black, J., dissented on the ground that the Labor Management Relations Act should not be construed so as to require an individual employee, after he is out of a job, to submit a claim involving wages to grievance and arbitration proceedings or to surrender his right to sue his employer in court for the enforcement of his claim.

COUNSEL

Samuel H. Burr argued the cause for petitioner. With him on the brief were Andrew J. Thomas and James R. Forman, Jr.

Richard L. Jones argued the cause for respondent. With him on the brief were John D. Prince, Jr., and Edwin L. Brobston.

J. Albert Woll, Robert C. Mayer, Theodore J. St. Antoine and Thomas E. Harris filed a brief for the American Federation of Labor and Congress of Industrial Organizations, as amicus curiae, urging reversal.

DAVIS

v

BALTIMORE & OHIO RAILROAD CO.

379 US 671, 13 L ed 2d 594, 85 S Ct 636

January 25, 1965

Decision: Evidence in FELA action held sufficient to sustain verdict for railroad employee.

SUMMARY

In a Federal Employers' Liability Act suit brought by a railroad tallyman and trucker in the Superior Court of Baltimore City, Maryland, there was conflicting testimony as to whether the employee mounted a forklift truck and backed it into an open elevator shaft, thereby sustaining his injuries, or was injured when the operator assigned to the truck negligently left it unattended, and it rolled toward and struck the employee, propelling him into the shaft and falling in on top of him. The jury found for the injured employee, and the Maryland Court of Appeals reversed on the ground that the jury's verdict was based on conjecture. (235 Md 568, 202 A2d 348.)

On certiorari, the Supreme Court of the United States reversed. In a per curiam opinion expressing the unanimous view of the Court, it was held that the Maryland Court of Appeals improperly invaded the function and province of the jury in a Federal Employers' Liability Act case.

Harlan, J., while stating that cases like the instant case "are not the proper business of this Court," joined the Court's opinion.

Stewart, J., expressed agreement with the views of Mr. Justice Harlan.

COUNSEL

B. Nathaniel Richter, Charles A. Lord and Amos I. Meyers for petitioner.

Fenton L. Martin for respondent.

STATE OF TEXAS, Plaintiff,

v

STATE OF NEW JERSEY et al.

379 US 674, 13 L ed 2d 596, 85 S Ct 626

Argued November 9, 1964.   Decided
February 1, 1965.

Decision: Unclaimed debts held subject to escheat only
by the state of the creditor's last-known address as
shown by the debtor's books and records.

SUMMARY

In an action brought in the Supreme Court of the
United States, Texas sued New Jersey, Pennsylvania, and
a corporation owing numerous unclaimed debts, for an
injunction and a declaration of rights as to which state
had jurisdiction to take title to the claims by escheat.
Florida intervened.

In an opinion by Black, J., expressing the views of
eight members of the Court, it was held that the claims
were subject to escheat only by the state of the last-
known address of the creditor, as shown by the corporate debtor's books and records, and that with respect
to property owed persons as to whom there was no record
of any address at all, or whose last-known address was
in a state not providing for escheat of the property owed
them, the property was subject to escheat by the state of
the corporate domicil, provided that another state could
later escheat upon proof that the last-known address
of the creditor was within its borders.

Stewart, J., dissented on the ground that only the state
of the debtor's incorporation has power to escheat in-

tangible property when the whereabouts of the creditor are unknown.

COUNSEL

W. O. Shultz II, Assistant Attorney General of Texas, argued the cause for plaintiff. With him on the brief was Waggoner Carr, Attorney General of Texas.

Charles J. Kehoe, Deputy Attorney General of New Jersey, argued the cause for the State of New Jersey, defendant. With him on the brief were Arthur J. Sills, Attorney General of New Jersey, and Theodore I. Botter, First Assistant Attorney General.

Fred M. Burns, Assistant Attorney General of Florida, argued the cause for the State of Florida, intervenor. With him on the brief were James W. Kynes, Attorney General of Florida, and Jack W. Harnett, Assistant Attorney General.

Joseph H. Resnick, Assistant Attorney General of Pennsylvania, argued the cause for the State of Pennsylvania, defendant.

Augustus S. Ballard argued the cause for the Sun Oil Company, defendant.

Ralph W. Oman argued the cause for the Life Insurance Association of America, as amicus curiae. On the brief were William B. McElhenny and Warren Elliott.

BLOW et al.

v

NORTH CAROLINA

379 US 684, 13 L ed 2d 603, 85 S Ct 635

February 1, 1965

Decision: Civil Rights Act of 1964 held to abate state trespass prosecutions of Negroes continuing to wait outside of restaurant notwithstanding owner's request to leave.

SUMMARY

Before the enactment of the Civil Rights Act of 1964, Negroes were convicted in a North Carolina state court of violating a state trespass statute by continuing to wait outside a racially discriminatory restaurant notwithstanding the owner's request to leave. Their convictions were affirmed by the Supreme Court of North Carolina. (261 NC 463, 135 SE2d 14; 261 NC 467, 135 SE2d 17.)

On certiorari, the Supreme Court of the United States vacated the judgments and ordered the indictments dismissed. In a per curiam opinion expressing the view of five members of the Court, the Court relied upon Hamm v Rock Hill (1964) 379 US 306, 13 L ed 2d 300, 85 S Ct 384, supra, p. 37.

Black, Harlan, and **White, JJ.,** dissented. They would affirm the judgments below for the reasons stated in the dissenting opinions in the Hamm Case.

Stewart, J., also dissented. He would vacate the judgment below and remand the case to that court for the reasons stated in his dissenting opinion in the Hamm Case.

COUNSEL

Jack Greenberg, Constance Baker Motley, James M. Nabrit III, Derrick A. Bell, Jr., Charles L. Black, Jr., Samuel S. Mitchell and Floyd B. McKissick for petitioners.

T. W. Bruton, Attorney General of North Carolina, and Ralph Moody, Deputy Attorney General, for respondent.

FEDERAL POWER COMMISSION,

v

AMERADA PETROLEUM CORP. et al.

379 US 687, 13 L ed 2d 605, 85 S Ct 632

Decided February 1, 1965

Decision: Natural gas sales held within Federal Power Commission's jurisdiction where gas was contractually restricted to intrastate use but part of it was in fact resold in interstate commerce as a result of commingling with other gas.

SUMMARY

Several years after a decision upholding the Federal Power Commission's refusal to assert jurisdiction over natural gas sales under certain contracts, the Commission asserted jurisdiction over natural gas sales under new contracts between the same parties, where the gas sold under the new contracts was commingled with gas destined for out-of-state resale. (30 FPC 200.) The United States Court of Appeals for the Eighth Circuit reversed on the grounds that the sales were beyond the Commission's jurisdiction and the parties were collaterally estopped by the previous decision from relitigating the question. (334 F2d 404.)

On certiorari, the Supreme Court of the United States reversed. In a per curiam opinion expressing the unanimous views of the Court, it was held that (1) the Commission had jurisdiction of the sales for the reasons stated in California v Lo-Vaca Gathering Co. (1965) 379 US 366, 13 L ed 2d 357, 85 S Ct 486, supra, p. 46, and (2) the rule of collateral estoppel was inapplicable because different events and transactions were involved, and no judgment governing past events was in jeopardy.

Goldberg, J., joined by Harlan and Stewart, JJ., joined in the Court's opinion and judgment, but stated that the decision did not reach the question whether in spite of original commingling there might be a separate non-jurisdictional transaction of a precise amount of gas.

COUNSEL

Solicitor General Cox, Richard A. Solomon, Howard E. Wahrenbrock, Robert L. Russell and Peter H. Schiff for petitioner.

William H. Webster, Edwin S. Nail and Joseph W. Morris for Amerada Petroleum Corp., and William R. Allen and Cecil E. Munn for Signal Oil & Gas Co., respondents.

STEWART L. UDALL, Secretary of the
Interior, Petitioner,

v

JAMES K. TALLMAN et al.

380 US 1, 13 L ed 2d 616, 85 S Ct 792

Argued October 22 and 26, 1964.

Decided March 1, 1965.

Decision: Secretary of Interior's reasonable interpretation of executive order and public land order as
not barring oil and gas leases on certain public lands
held entitled to credence by courts.

SUMMARY

In an action in the nature of mandamus instituted
in the United States District Court for the District of
Columbia, persons whose applications for oil and gas
leases in the Kenai National Moose Range in Alaska
were rejected by the Department of the Interior, on
the ground that the lands had been leased to prior applicants, asserted that the prior applications were ineffective
because the lands were closed to leasing by virtue of
Executive Order No. 8979 and Public Land Order No.
487, when the prior applications were filed. The District
Court dismissed the complaint, but the United States
Court of Appeals for the District of Columbia reversed.
(116 App DC 379, 324 F2d 411.)

On certiorari, the Supreme Court of the United States
reversed. In an opinion by Warren, Ch. J., expressing
the unanimous views of the Court, it was held that since
the Secretary's interpretation of the orders as not barring
leases was reasonable, consistently applied, and a repeated

matter of public record, and since leases had been developed in reliance upon it, the courts must give it credence.

Douglas and **Harlan, JJ.**, did not participate.

COUNSEL

Wayne G. Barnett argued the cause for petitioner. With him on the briefs were Solicitor General Cox, Roger P. Marquis and Edmund B. Clark.

Charles F. Wheatley, Jr., argued the cause for respondents. With him on the brief was Robert L. McCarty.

Briefs of amici curiae, urging reversal, were filed by Clayton L. Orn, Marvin J. Sonosky, Oscar L. Chapman, Martin L. Friedman and Marion B. Plant for Marathon Oil Company et al., and by Abe Fortas, Joseph A. Ball, Gordon A. Goodwin, Francis R. Kirkham, Turner H. McBaine and Clark M. Clifford for Richfield Oil Corporation et al.

MORTIMER SINGER, Petitioner,

v

UNITED STATES

380 US 25, 13 L ed 2d 630, 85 S Ct 783

Argued November 18, 1964. Decided
March 1, 1965.

Decision: Federal Criminal Procedure Rule 23(a), conditioning defendant's waiver of jury trial upon court's approval and government's consent, held valid.

SUMMARY

On the opening day of defendant's trial, in the United States District Court for the Southern District of California, on charges of violations of the mail fraud statute, defendant offered in writing to waive a trial by jury for the purpose of shortening the trial. The trial court was willing to approve the waiver, but the government refused to give its consent under Federal Criminal Procedure Rule 23(a), which conditions a defendant's waiver of a jury trial upon both the court's approval and the government's consent. Defendant was subsequently convicted by a jury and the Court of Appeals for the Ninth Circuit affirmed. (326 F2d 132.)

On certiorari, the United States Supreme Court affirmed. In an opinion by **Warren, Ch. J.,** expressing the unanimous view of the Court, it was held that the Federal Constitution neither confers nor recognizes the right of criminal defendants to have their cases tried before a judge alone, and that consequently Rule 23(a) is valid.

COUNSEL

Sidney Dorfman argued the cause and filed a brief for petitioner.

Beatrice Rosenberg argued the cause for the United States. With her on the brief were Solicitor General Cox, Assistant Attorney General Miller and Sidney M. Glazer.

Briefs of amici curiae were filed by Victor Rabinowitz and Leonard Boudin for Joni Rabinowitz, and by Justin A. Stanley for Nicholas Jacop Uselding.

———————

THOMAS J. CRIDER, Petitioner,

v

ZURICH INSURANCE COMPANY

380 US 39, 13 L ed 2d 641, 85 S Ct 769

Argued January 19, 1965. Decided
March 1, 1965.

Decision: Courts of Alabama, where an Alabama resident in employ of a Georgia corporation was injured, held not precluded by full faith and credit clause from entertaining employee's action based on Georgia Workmen's Compensation Act, even though that act affords a remedy only in the Georgia Compensation Board.

SUMMARY

Plaintiff, a resident of Alabama injured there while in the employ of a Georgia corporation, sued in an Alabama state court under the Georgia Workmen's Compensation Act and obtained a default judgment against his employer's insurer. He then brought the instant action against the insurer in the United States District Court for the Northern District of Alabama to enforce the default judgment. The District Court granted defendant's motion to dismiss (224 F Supp 87) and the Court of Appeals for the Fifth Circuit affirmed (324 F2d 499).

On certiorari, the United States Supreme Court reversed. In an opinion by Douglas, J., expressing the view of six members of the Court, it was held that the full faith and credit clause did not preclude the Alabama court from entertaining the action based on the Georgia Workmen's Compensation Act, even though that act was "an exclusive one," providing for primary jurisdiction in the Georgia Compensation Board and precluding original court jurisdiction.

Goldberg, J., joined by Harlan and Stewart, JJ., dissented, on the ground that it was not necessary for the Court to decide the constitutional issue, since the dismissal of the action by the courts below was based on independent state law and not on federal grounds, and in any event was supported by independent Alabama law. He would dismiss the writ of certiorari as improvidently granted, and in any event vacate the judgment below and remand the case to the District Court for clarification of its opinion as to the status of Alabama law.

COUNSEL

Max C. Pope, pro hac vice, by special leave of Court, argued the cause for petitioner. With him on the brief was J. Terry Huffstutler.

Foster Etheredge argued the cause and filed a brief for respondent.

———————————

RONALD L. FREEDMAN, Appellant,

v

STATE OF MARYLAND

380 US 51, 13 L ed 2d 649, 85 S Ct 734

Argued November 19, 1964. Decided
March 1, 1965.

Decision: Maryland motion-picture censorship statute
held invalid because of its failure to provide adequate
safeguards against undue inhibition of protected expression.

SUMMARY

In a criminal prosecution in a Maryland state court
for violation of a provision in the Maryland motion-
picture censorship statute making it unlawful to exhibit
a motion picture without having obtained a license, defendant contended that the statute in its entirety unconstitutionally impaired freedom of expression. Defendant
was convicted, and the Court of Appeals of Maryland
affirmed. (233 Md 498, 197 A2d 232.)

On appeal, the Supreme Court of the United States
reversed. In an opinion by **Brennan, J.**, expressing the
views of seven members of the Court, it was held that
defendant had standing to attack the statute, and that
while motion pictures are not necessarily subject to the
precise rules governing any other particular method of
expression, the Maryland statute violated the constitutional guaranty of freedom of expression because under
the statute (1) upon the censor's disapproval of the film,
the exhibitor must assume the burden of instituting judicial proceedings and of persuading the courts that the
film is protected expression, (2) once the censor has acted
against a film, exhibition is prohibited pending judicial

review, however protracted, and (3) no assurance of prompt judicial determination is afforded.

Douglas, J., joined by Black, J., concurred, expressing the view that motion pictures are entitled to the same degree and kind of protection under the First Amendment as other forms of expression, and hence are entitled to be free from censorship.

COUNSEL

Thomas B. Finan, Attorney General of Maryland, argued the cause for appellee. With him on the brief were Robert F. Sweeney and Roger D. Redden, Assistant Attorneys General.

Edward De Grazia and Melvin L. Wulf filed a brief for the American Civil Liberties Union et al., as amici curiae, urging reversal.

UNITED STATES, Petitioner,

v

JACKIE HAMILTON GAINEY

380 US 63, 13 L ed 2d 658, 85 S Ct 754

Argued October 15, 1964. Decided
March 1, 1965.

Decision: Inference, authorized by 26 USC § 5601(b)
(2), of guilt of conducting illegal distillery from fact
of accused's unexplained presence at illegal still,
held constitutional.

SUMMARY

During a prosecution in the United States District
Court for the Middle District of Georgia, for carrying
on an illegal distillery business, the court instructed the
jury in accordance with 26 USC § 5601(b)(2) that the
accused's unexplained presence at the site of an illegal
distillery business is sufficient evidence to authorize conviction of the offense, unless the accused explains his
presence to the satisfaction of the jury. The United
States Court of Appeals for the Fifth Circuit reversed
the accused's convictions on the ground that the statutory inference was unconstitutional. (322 F2d 292.)

On certiorari, the Supreme Court of the United States
reversed. In an opinion by Stewart, J., expressing the
views of seven members of the Court, it was held that
the statutory inference (1) is constitutional; (2) does
not require a judge to submit a case to the jury, or preclude the grant of a judgment notwithstanding the verdict, where the only evidence is of presence; and (3)
does not require a jury to convict if they find that the
government has not proved guilt beyond a reasonable
doubt.

Black, J., dissented on the ground that the statute is unconstitutional and that the construction of the statute in (2), supra, is an "emasculation" of the statute.

Douglas, J., dissented on the ground that the trial court's charge violated the privilege against self-incrimination by making an improper comment on the accused's failure to testify.

COUNSEL

Louis F. Claiborne argued the cause for the United States. With him on the brief were Solicitor General Cox, Assistant Attorney General Miller, Beatrice Rosenberg and Jerome M. Feit.

Joseph H. Davis argued the cause for respondent. With him on the brief was J. Sewell Elliott.

SERGEANT HERBERT N. CARRINGTON,
Petitioner,

v

ALAN V. RASH et al.

380 US 89, 13 L ed 2d 675, 85 S Ct 775

Argued January 28, 1965. Decided
March 1, 1965.

Decision: Provision in Texas Constitution which denies
a serviceman the right to vote on the sole ground
of his status as serviceman held to violate equal
protection clause.

SUMMARY

The petitioner, a sergeant in the United States Army,
who after entering the service had acquired a bona fide
domicil in Texas, instituted an original mandamus proceeding in the Supreme Court of Texas to require his local
election officials to permit him to vote. The issue was
whether a provision of the Texas Constitution prohibiting
any member of the Armed Forces of the United States
who moved his home to Texas during the course of
his military duty from ever voting in any election in that
state so long as he was a member of the Armed Forces
deprived petitioner of a right secured by the equal protection clause of the Fourteenth Amendment. The Supreme Court of Texas decided that it did not and refused
to issue the writ, two justices dissenting. (378 SW2d
304.)

On certiorari, the Supreme Court of the United States
reversed. In an opinion by **Stewart, J.,** expressing the
view of seven members of the Court, it was held that
the provision of the Texas Constitution, as applied to
a bona fide domiciliary of Texas, violated the equal
protection clause.

[Supreme Ct Sum]—7

Harlan, J., dissented on the grounds that (1) the equal protection clause was not intended to touch state electoral matters, and (2) in any event the differentiation in voting eligibility requirements between those who came voluntarily into Texas and those ordered into Texas by military authority was founded on a rational classification.

Warren, Ch. J., did not participate.

COUNSEL

Wayne Windle argued the cause for petitioner. With him on the briefs was W. C. Peticolas.

Hawthorne Phillips, First Assistant Attorney General of Texas, and Mary K. Wall, Assistant Attorney General, argued the cause for respondents. With them on the brief was Waggoner Carr, Attorney General of Texas.

UNITED STATES, Petitioner,

v

GIACOMO VENTRESCA

380 US 102, 13 L ed 2d 684, 85 S Ct 741

Argued January 18 and 19, 1965.

Decided March 1, 1965.

Decision: Search warrant held valid where issued on affidavit detailing facts observed in all significant respects by government investigators.

SUMMARY

A conviction of possessing and operating an illegal distillery was obtained in the United States District Court for Massachusetts after a still was found during a search under a warrant issued on the basis of a government investigator's detailed affidavit based on his own observations, information received by other government investigators, and reports made to the affiant describing the results of their observations and investigations. The United States Court of Appeals for the First Circuit reversed on the ground that the affidavit was insufficient to establish probable cause because it failed to indicate which of the facts alleged were hearsay and which were within the affiant's own knowledge. (324 F2d 864.)

On certiorari, the Supreme Court of the United States reversed. In an opinion by Goldberg, J., expressing the views of seven members of the Court, it was held that, properly read in a common sense rather than a technical way, the affidavit showed ample facts to establish probable cause and could not fairly be regarded as reflecting observations made in any significant part by persons other than government investigators.

Douglas, J., joined by **Warren**, Ch. J., dissented on the ground that the affidavit failed to identify the sources of the information.

COUNSEL

Frank I. Goodman argued the cause for the United States. On the brief were Solicitor General Cox, Assistant Attorney General Miller, Beatrice Rosenberg and Ronald L. Gainer.

Matthew R. McCann argued the cause for respondent. With him on the brief was Edward C. Maher.

LOUISIANA et al., Appellants,

v

UNITED STATES

380 US 145, 13 L ed 2d 709, 85 S Ct 817

Argued January 26 and 27, 1965.
Decided March 8, 1965.

Decision: Louisiana voting registration test, requiring
applicants to interpret federal and state constitutions
to satisfaction of voting registrars, held unconstitutional.

SUMMARY

The United States sued the state of Louisiana and
four of its voting officials in the United States District
Court for the Eastern District of Louisiana, alleging discrimination against Negro applicants for registration in
21 parishes by the application of an "interpretation test"
under which applicants were required to interpret any
section of the state or federal constitution when read to
them by a voting registrar. After the suit was filed, the
state board of registration adopted an allegedly objective
"citizenship test" to be applied only to new voter applicants. A three-judge District Court (1) held the interpretation test invalid, (2) ordered that use of the
citizenship test be postponed, in the 21 parishes where
the interpretation test had been followed, until there was
a complete reregistration of voters, so that the citizenship
test could apply alike to all or to none, (3) retained jurisdiction of the case, and (4) ordered that monthly reports
be filed concerning voting registration in the 21 parishes.
(225 F Supp 353.)

On direct appeal, the Supreme Court of the United
States affirmed. In an opinion by **Black, J.,** expressing

the views of eight members of the Court, it was held that the "interpretation test" was violative of the Fourteenth and Fifteenth Amendments, and of 42 USC § 1971(a), and that the District Court's decree was proper in all respects.

Harlan, J., stated separately that the majority's constitutional conclusions could be rested only on the Fifteenth Amendment, but that in all other respects he subscribed to the majority opinion.

COUNSEL

Harry J. Kron, Jr., Assistant Attorney General of Louisiana, argued the cause for appellants. With him on the brief were Jack P. F. Gremillion, Attorney General of Louisiana, and Carroll Buck, First Assistant Attorney General.

Louis F. Claiborne argued the cause for the United States. With him on the brief were Solicitor General Cox, Assistant Attorney General Marshall, Harold H. Greene and David Rubin.

UNITED STATES, Appellant,

v

MISSISSIPPI et al.

380 US 128, 13 L ed 2d 717, 85 S Ct 808

Argued January 26, 1965. Decided
March 8, 1965.

Decision: 42 USC § 1971, permitting suits by United States to protect Negroes' voting rights, held constitutional, and state held suable thereunder.

SUMMARY

In an action brought in the United States District Court for the Southern District of Mississippi, the United States sued the state of Mississippi, three state election commissioners, and six county voter registrars, alleging that they were engaged in acts hampering and destroying the right of Negro citizens of Mississippi to vote, principally by discriminatory application of state laws requiring voters to interpret the Mississippi Constitution, demonstrate an understanding of a citizen's duties, and show good moral character. A three-judge District Court dismissed the complaint on the grounds that the United States could not maintain such an action, the state could not be made a party defendant, the election commissioners lacked sufficient interest in enforcing the state laws to permit making them parties defendant, venue was improper as to the registrars, and the complaint failed to state a claim on which relief could be granted. (229 F Supp 925.)

On direct appeal, the Supreme Court of the United States reversed. In an opinion by **Black, J.,** expressing the views of eight members of the Court, it was held that (1) the suit was authorized by 42 USC § 1971, which is a constitutional exercise of powers conferred by the Fifteenth Amendment; (2) the Eleventh Amendment does not render a state immune from suit by the United States; (3) the defendants were properly joined, and venue was properly laid; and (4) the complaint stated a cause of action.

Harlan, J., stated separately that the majority's constitutional conclusions could be rested only on the Fifteenth Amendment, but in all other respects he fully subscribed to the majority opinion.

COUNSEL

Solicitor General Cox argued the cause for the United States. With him on the brief were Assistant Attorney General Marshall, Louis F. Claiborne, Harold H. Greene, David Rubin, Howard A. Glickstein and J. Harold Flannery.

Charles Clark, Special Assistant Attorney General of Mississippi, argued the cause for appellees. With him on the briefs were Joe T. Patterson, Attorney General of Mississippi, Dugas Shands, Assistant Attorney General, P. M. Stockett, Special Assistant Attorney General, and Aubrey Bell.

Francis Biddle, Norman Dorsen and Melvin L. Wulf filed a brief for the American Civil Liberties Union, as amicus curiae, urging reversal.

UNITED STATES, Appellant,

v

BOSTON AND MAINE RAILROAD et al.

380 US 157, 13 L ed 2d 728, 85 S Ct 868

Argued January 21, 1965. Decided March 8, 1965.

Decision: Railroad's officers who agree to assist another corporation to obtain profits by purchasing railroad's coaches and who receive substantial monies from purchasing corporation pursuant to agreement, held not to have "substantial interest" in purchasing corporation within meaning of § 10 of Clayton Act.

SUMMARY

In a federal criminal proceeding in the District Court of Massachusetts, count I of the indictment charged that a railroad and three of its officers violated § 10 of the Clayton Act by the railroad's sale of 10 coaches, valued in excess of $50,000, to another corporation, in which the railroad's three officers had a "substantial interest," competitive bidding not having been used. A bill of particulars described the officers' "substantial interest" in the purchasing corporation as consisting of an agreement for the purpose of producing profits for the purchasing corporation from dealings by it in property acquired from the railroad through the assistance of the three officers and pursuant to which the officers were to and did receive substantial moneys. Granting motions to dismiss count I, the District Court held that § 10 was limited to one who had a present legal interest in the purchasing corporation and did not include one whose only interest was in the outcome of what may have been an illegal and illicit plan to siphon off for his personal benefit property of the railroad through the medium of the purchasing corporation. (225 F Supp 577.)

On direct appeal, the United States Supreme Court vacated and remanded the case, giving the government an opportunity to file an amended bill of particulars in the District Court. In an opinion by **Douglas, J.,** expressing the unanimous view of the Court, it was held that the District Court properly concluded that the defendants' conduct, as alleged in the bill of particulars, was not within the scope of § 10; but it was also held that the District Court's construction of § 10 had been too narrow and that the words "substantial interest in such other corporation," as used in § 10, presupposed either an existing investment in the corporation, or the creation of the corporation for one's own use, or a joint venture or continued course of dealings with the corporation for profit sharing.

COUNSEL

Robert B. Hummel argued the cause for the United States. With him on the briefs were Solicitor General Cox, Assistant Attorney General Orrick and John H. Dougherty.

Edward O. Proctor, Sr., argued the cause for appellees. On the brief for appellee Boston & Maine Railroad was Edward B. Hanify. With Mr. Proctor on the brief for appellees McGinnis et al. were William T. Griffin, Lothrop Withington and John M. Reed.

UNITED STATES, Petitioner,

v

DANIEL ANDREW SEEGER (No. 50)

UNITED STATES, Petitioner,

v

ARNO SASCHA JAKOBSON (No. 51)

FOREST BRITT PETER, Petitioner,

v

UNITED STATES (No. 29)

380 US 163, 13 L ed 2d 733, 85 S Ct 850

Argued November 16 and 17, 1964.
Decided March 8, 1965.

Decision: Defendants in criminal prosecution for refusing to submit to induction in the Armed Forces held conscientious objectors exempt from military service, notwithstanding their unorthodox beliefs as to Supreme Being.

SUMMARY

The present cases involved the construction of the provision of § 6(j) of the Universal Military Training and Service Act of 1948 which, as a prerequisite of exempting a conscientious objector from military service, requires his belief in a relation to a Supreme Being involving duties superior to those arising from any human relation. In No. 50 defendant's claim to exemption as conscientious objector was denied after he, professing religious belief

and faith and not disavowing, although not clearly demonstrating, any belief in a relation to a Supreme Being,
stated that "the cosmic order does, perhaps, suggest a
creative intelligence" and decried the tremendous "spir-
itual" price man must pay for his willingness to destroy
human life. He was convicted in the District Court for
the Southern District of New York of having refused to
submit to induction in the Armed Forces. His conviction
was reversed by the Court of Appeals for the Second Circuit. (326 F2d 846.) In No. 51 the registrant stated
that he believed in a "Supreme Being" who was "Creator
of Man" in the sense of being "ultimately responsible for
the existence of" man and who was "the Supreme Real-
ity" of which "the existence of man is the result." He was
convicted in the same District Court of the same offense,
and his conviction was also reversed by the Court of Appeals for the Second Circuit. (325 F2d 409.) In No. 29
the registrant, although hedging the question as to his
belief in a Supreme Being, acknowledged "some power
manifest in nature . . . the supreme expression" that
helps man in ordering his life. He was also convicted of
the same offense in the United States District Court for
the Northern District of California and his conviction was
affirmed by the Court of Appeals for the Ninth Circuit.
(324 F2d 173.)

On writs of certiorari, the United States Supreme Court
affirmed the judgments in Nos. 50 and 51, and reversed
the judgment in No. 29. In an opinion by Clark, J.,
expressing the unanimous views of the Court, it was held
that (1) the statute, in using the expression "Supreme
Being" rather than the designation "God," was merely
clarifying the meaning of religious training and belief so
as to embrace all religions and to exclude essentially
political, sociological, or philosophical views, (2) under
this construction the test of belief "in a relation to a Supreme Being" is whether a given belief that is sincere and

meaningful occupies a place in the life of its possessor parallel to that filled by the orthodox belief in God of one who clearly qualifies for the exemption, and (3) the registrants in all three cases met this test.

Douglas, J., concurred in a separate opinion, expressing the view that a construction of the statute contrary to the one adopted by the Court, would violate the "free exercise clause" of the First Amendment and would result in a denial of equal protection by preferring some religions over others.

COUNSEL

Solicitor General Cox argued the cause for the United States in all cases. Assistant Attorney General Miller was with him on the briefs in all cases. Ralph S. Spritzer was with him on the briefs in Nos. 50 and 51, and Marshall Tamor Golding was with him on the briefs in No. 50.

Duane B. Beeson argued the cause and filed a brief for petitioner in No. 29.

Kenneth A. Greenawalt argued the cause and filed a brief for respondent in No. 50.

Herman Adlerstein argued the cause and filed a brief for respondent in No. 51.

Briefs of amici curiae, urging affirmance in Nos. 50 and 51 and reversal in No. 29, were filed by Alfred Lawrence Toombs and Melvin L. Wulf for the American Civil Liberties Union, and by Leo Pfeffer, Shad Polier, Will Maslow and Joseph B. Robison for the American Jewish Congress. Briefs of amici curiae, urging affirmance in No. 50 were filed by Herbert A. Wolff, Leo Rosen, Nanette Dembitz and Nancy F. Wechsler for the American Ethical Union, and by Tolbert H. McCarroll, Lester Forest and Paul Blanshard for the American Humanist Association.

DEPARTMENT OF MENTAL HYGIENE OF CALIFORNIA, Petitioner,

v

EVELYN KIRCHNER, Administratrix of the Estate of Ellinor Green Vance

380 US 194, 13 L ed 2d 753, 85 S Ct 871

Argued January 19, 1965.   Decided
March 8, 1965.

Decision: Judgment of California Supreme Court invalidating state statute imposing liability upon estate or relatives of mentally ill persons for their support in state institution vacated and case remanded for clarification of basis of decision as resting on Federal or state Constitution.

SUMMARY

The California Department of Mental Hygiene filed a suit against the administratrix of a deceased person's estate to recover amounts spent by the department for the deceased, the mother of the administratrix, while the mother was cared for in a state institution. The claim was based on a California statute imposing liability upon the estate or relatives of mentally ill persons for their support in a state institution. The trial court rendered judgment on the pleadings. The California District Court of Appeal affirmed (Cal App) (29 Cal Rptr 312), but the Supreme Court of California reversed, finding that the statute violated "the basic constitutional guaranty of equal protection of the law" (60 Cal 2d 716, 36 Cal Rptr 488, 388 P2d 720).

On certiorari, the United States Supreme Court vacated the judgment below and remanded the case to the

California Supreme Court. In an opinion by **Harlan, J.**, expressing the views of eight members of the Court, the decision was rested on the ground that the United States Supreme Court had no jurisdiction, because it was unable to ascertain from the opinion of the court below whether its decision was rested on the equal protection clause of the Fourteenth Amendment or the equivalent provision of the California Constitution, or both.

Douglas, J., believing it clear that the California Supreme Court did not rest its decision solely on the Fourteenth Amendment, would dismiss the writ.

COUNSEL

Elizabeth Palmer, Deputy Attorney General of California, argued the cause for petitioner. With her on the briefs were Thomas C. Lynch, Attorney General of California, Harold B. Haas, Assistant Attorney General, and John Carl Porter and Asher Rubin, Deputy Attorneys General.

Alan A. Dougherty argued the cause for respondent. With him on the brief was John Walton Dinkelspiel.

Briefs of amici curiae, urging reversal, were filed by William G. Clark, Attorney General of Illinois, Richard E. Friedman, First Assistant Attorney General, Richard A. Michael, Assistant Attorney General, and Jerome F. Goldberg and John E. Coons, Special Assistant Attorneys General, for the State of Illinois; by William B. Saxbe, Attorney General of Ohio, and Joanne Wharton, Assistant Attorney General, for the State of Ohio; by Robert Y. Thornton, Attorney General of Oregon, and A. Duane Pinkerton and Neil C. Hoyez, Assistant Attorneys General, for the State of Oregon; and by John J. O'Connell, Attorney General of Washington, and Stephen C. Way, Assistant Attorney General, for the State of Washington.

Briefs of amici curiae, urging affirmance, were filed by Robert W. Kenny for the National Federation of the Blind and the California League of Senior Citizens, and by A. Kenneth Pye, John R. Schmertz, Jr., and Bernard D. Fischman for the National Association for Retarded Children, Inc., and the American Orthopsychiatric Association.

ROBERT SWAIN, Petitioner,

v

STATE OF ALABAMA

380 US 202, 13 L ed 2d 759, 85 S Ct 824

Argued December 8, 1964.   Decided
March 8, 1965.

Decision: Prosecutor's use of peremptory strikes to eliminate Negroes from jury held not to deny equal protection of laws to Negro defendant.

SUMMARY

A Negro convicted of rape by an all-white jury in the
Circuit Court of Talladega County, Alabama, appealed
from his conviction, asserting that he was denied equal
protection of the laws by discriminatory jury selection in
three respects: (1) discrimination in the selection of
venires, demonstrated by the fact that while 26 percent
of the persons eligible for jury duty were Negroes, the
venires contained only 10 to 15 percent Negroes; (2)
discrimination in the selection of jurors from the veniremen, demonstrated by the fact that the prosecutor used
his peremptory strikes in the present case to remove all
Negro veniremen; and (3) discrimination in the use of
the peremptory strike system in Talladega County
through the years, perverting its purpose in a scheme to
exclude all Negroes from ever serving on petit juries there
by the prosecutors' striking all Negro veniremen, demonstrated by the fact that no Negro had ever served on a
petit jury in Talladega County. The Alabama Supreme
Court affirmed the conviction. (275 Ala 508, 156 So 2d
368.)

On certiorari, the Supreme Court of the United States

affirmed. In an opinion by **White, J.,** expressing the
views of five members of the Court, it was held that (1)
an accused is not constitutionally entitled to a propor-
tionate number of his race on the jury which tries him,
and the underrepresentation of his race by 10 percent
does not show purposeful discrimination; (2) in a particular case, a prosecutor may constitutionally use his peremptory strikes to eliminate all of the accused's race from
the jury; and (3) the fact that no Negroes had ever served
on a petit jury in Talladega County did not show a per-
version of a peremptory strike system by the prosecution
where the record failed to show when, how often, and
under what circumstances the prosecutor alone had been
responsible for striking Negro veniremen.

Harlan, J., joined in the Court's opinion but emphasized that the Court did not decide the constitutionality
of the alleged practice discussed in (3).

Black, J., concurred in the result.

Goldberg, J., joined by **Warren, Ch. J.,** and **Douglas, J.,**
dissented from (3) on the ground that the evidence made
out a prima facie case of unlawful jury exclusion, placing
on the state the burden of proving that the exclusion resulted from reasons other than racial discrimination.

COUNSEL

Constance Baker Motley argued the cause for petitioner. With her on the brief were Jack Greenberg,
James M. Nabrit III, Orzell Billingsley, Jr., Peter A. Hall
and Michael Meltsner.

Leslie Hall, Assistant Attorney General of Alabama,
argued the cause for respondent. With him on the brief
was Richmond M. Flowers, Attorney General of Alabama.

RADIO AND TELEVISION BROADCAST TECHNICIANS LOCAL UNION 1264,

etc., et al., Petitioners,

v

BROADCAST SERVICE OF MOBILE, Inc.

380 US 255, 13 L ed 2d 789, 85 S Ct 876

Argued March 2 and 3, 1965. Decided March 15, 1965.

Decision: State court held without jurisdiction of suit to enjoin union picketing and boycott of radio station constituting part of integrated enterprise meeting NLRB jurisdictional standards.

SUMMARY

A radio station sued a union in the Circuit Court of Mobile County, Alabama, to enjoin the union's peaceful picketing and its solicitation of advertisers aimed at persuading them to cease doing business with the station. The Circuit Court dissolved a temporary injunction on the ground that its jurisdiction was pre-empted by the National Labor Relations Act. The Supreme Court of Alabama reversed, declaring that the state court had jurisdiction because the union failed to allege that the station's annual gross business exceeded $100,000. (276 Ala 93, 159 So 2d 452.)

On certiorari, the Supreme Court of the United States reversed. In a per curiam opinion expressing the unanimous view of the Court, it was held that the state courts lacked jurisdiction because the station was part of an integrated enterprise having gross receipts in excess of $100,000 per year.

COUNSEL

J. R. Goldthwaite, Jr., argued the cause and filed a brief for petitioners.

Willis C. Darby, Jr., argued the cause for respondent. With him on the brief was George E. Stone, Jr.

Solicitor General Cox, Arnold Ordman, Dominick L. Manoli and Norton J. Come filed a brief for the United States, as amicus curiae, urging reversal.

TEXTILE WORKERS UNION OF
AMERICA, Petitioner,

v

DARLINGTON MANUFACTURING COMPANY
et al. (No. 37)

NATIONAL LABOR RELATIONS BOARD,
Petitioner,

v

DARLINGTON MANUFACTURING COMPANY
et al. (No. 41)

380 US 263, 13 L ed 2d 827, 85 S Ct 994

Argued December 9, 1964. Decided
March 29, 1965.

Decision: Under National Labor Relations Act, employer
held to have absolute right to close his entire business, but not part of his business.

SUMMARY

A majority of the stock of a textile manufacturing company was owned by a textile selling house, which was
controlled by the manufacturing company's president and
his family and which operated 17 textile manufacturers
and marketed the products manufactured in 27 different
mills. During a union organizational campaign, the
manufacturing company threatened to close its one mill
if the union won a representation election. Shortly after
the union won the election, the mill ceased operations, all
its employees were discharged, and all of its machinery
and equipment was sold piecemeal at auction. The union
filed unfair labor practice charges with the National
Labor Relations Board, which found that the company

had been closed because of the antiunion animus of its president and that the closing constituted a violation of § 8(a)(3) of the National Labor Relations Act, prohibiting discrimination by an employer to discourage union membership. (139 NLRB 241.) The Board also found that the company was part of a single integrated employer group controlled by its president's family through the selling house, and that the selling house could be held liable for the company's unfair labor practice. Alternatively, the Board found that since the company was a part of the selling house's enterprise, the selling house had violated the Act by closing part of its business for a discriminatory purpose. The Board ordered backpay for all of the company's employees until they obtained substantially equivalent work or were put on preferential hiring lists at the selling house's other mills, and the selling house was ordered to bargain with the union in regard to details of compliance with the order. On review, the Court of Appeals for the Fourth Circuit set aside the Board's order, holding that even if the selling house had the status of a single employer, an employer has the absolute right to close out a part or all of its business regardless of antiunion motives. (325 F2d 682.)

On certiorari, the United States Supreme Court ordered the case remanded to the National Labor Relations Board for further findings as to the purpose and effect of the closing of the mill. In an opinion by Harlan, J., expressing the views of seven members of the Court, it was held that the closing of an employer's entire business, even if motivated by vindictiveness toward the union, is not an unfair labor practice, but that a partial closing is an unfair labor practice if motivated by a purpose to chill unionism in any of the remaining plants of the single employer, and if the employer may reasonably have foreseen that such closing will likely have that effect.

Stewart and **Goldberg**, JJ., did not participate.

COUNSEL

Irving Abramson argued the cause for petitioner in No. 37. With him on the brief were Everett E. Lewis, Donald Grody and Leonard Greenwald.

Dominick L. Manoli argued the cause for petitioner in No. 41. With him on the briefs were Solicitor General Cox, Arnold Ordman, Norton J. Come and Nancy M. Sherman.

Sam J. Ervin, Jr., and Stuart N. Updike argued the cause for respondents in both cases. With Mr. Ervin on the brief for Darlington Manufacturing Co. was Thornton H. Brooks. With Mr. Updike on the brief for Deering Milliken, Inc., were John Lord O'Brian, Hugh B. Cox and John R. Schoemer, Jr.

J. Albert Woll, Robert C. Mayer, Theodore J. St. Antoine and Thomas E. Harris filed a brief for the American Federation of Labor and Congress of Industrial Organizations, as amicus curiae, urging reversal.

Briefs of amici curiae, urging affirmance, were filed by Rowland F. Kirks for the American Textile Manufacturers Institute, and by Gerard D. Reilly for the Chamber of Commerce of the United States.

NATIONAL LABOR RELATIONS BOARD,
Petitioner,

v

JOHN BROWN et al.

380 US 278, 13 L ed 2d 839, 85 S Ct 980

Argued January 19, 1965. Decided
March 29, 1965.

Decision: Lockout and continuation of business through
temporary replacements, by nonstruck members of
multiemployer retail store bargaining group, held
not unfair labor practices where struck employer-
member also so continued operations.

SUMMARY

When a union which had bargained with a multiemployer retail store group struck one of the stores, which
continued business with temporary replacements, the
other stores locked out all employees represented by the
union and continued business in the same way. The
National Labor Relations Board held that the nonstruck
employers were guilty of unfair labor practices under
§ 8(a)(1) and (3) of the amended National Labor Relations Act (137 NLRB 73), but the United States Court
of Appeals for the Tenth Circuit refused to enforce the
Board's order (319 F2d 7).

On certiorari, the Supreme Court of the United States
affirmed. In an opinion by Brennan, J., expressing the
views of six members of the Court, it was held that (1)
the lockout was legal; (2) the nonstruck stores' continuation of business served a legitimate business purpose, and
was lawful absent a showing of antiunion animus; and
(3) there was no showing of such animus.

Goldberg, J., joined by **Warren, Ch. J.,** concurring, stated that a different case would be presented if the replacements were permanent.

White, J., dissented on the grounds that the nonstruck employers had no unqualified right to lock out union employees and, by hiring nonunion replacements, were guilty of unfair labor practices.

COUNSEL

Norton J. Come argued the cause for petitioner. With him on the brief were Solicitor General Cox, Arnold Ordman, Dominick L. Manoli, Gary Green and Nathan Lewin.

William L. Keller argued the cause for respondents. With him on the brief was Allen Butler.

S. G. Lippman and Tim L. Bornstein filed a brief for the Retail Clerks International Association, as amicus curiae, urging reversal.

Joseph M. McLaughlin and Frederick A. Morgan filed a brief for Food Employers Council, Inc., et al., as amici curiae, urging affirmance.

AMERICAN SHIP BUILDING COMPANY, Petitioner,

v

NATIONAL LABOR RELATIONS BOARD

380 US 300, 13 L ed 2d 855, 85 S Ct 955

Argued January 21, 1965. Decided
March 29, 1965.

Decision: Employer held not guilty of unfair labor practices in temporarily shutting down plant and laying off employees to exert economic pressure in support of legitimate bargaining position after bargaining impasse had been reached.

SUMMARY

An operator of four Great Lakes shipyards reached a bargaining impasse with unions representing his employees, and when the parties separated after the expiration of the existing contract, the operator, being apprehensive of a work stoppage when circumstances gave the unions increased strike leverage, completely shut down one shipyard, laid off all but two employees at another shipyard, and gradually laid off employees at a third shipyard. The National Labor Relations Board concluded that the layoffs violated § 8(a)(1) and (3) of the amended National Labor Relations Act. (142 NLRB 1362.) The United States Court of Appeals for the District of Columbia enforced the Board's order. (— App DC —, 331 F2d 839.)

On certiorari, the Supreme Court of the United States reversed. In an opinion by Stewart, J., expressing the views of six members of the Court, it was held that an employer does not violate § 8(a)(1) or (3) where, after a bargaining impasse has been reached, he temporarily shuts down his plant and lays off his employees for the sole purpose of bringing economic pressure to bear in support of his legitimate bargaining position.

White, J., concurring in the result, stated that the facts did not show a bargaining lockout, but merely a layoff for lack of work because the operator's customers feared a strike, and that the legality of a bargaining lockout is determined by balancing conflicting legitimate interests.

Goldberg, J., joined by **Warren, Ch. J.**, concurring in the result, stated that the employer's fear of a strike was reasonable and therefore the lockout was justified, but that, absent antiunion animus, in a § 8(a)(1) or (3) case the legality of an employer's conduct requires balancing conflicting legitimate interests.

COUNSEL

William S. Tyson argued the cause for petitioner. With him on the brief was Charles Cavano.

Norton J. Come argued the cause for respondent. With him on the brief were Solicitor General Cox, Frank Goodman, Arnold Ordman and Dominick L. Manoli.

William B. Barton filed a brief for the Chamber of Commerce of the United States, as amicus curiae, urging reversal.

Briefs of amici curiae, urging affirmance, were filed by J. Albert Woll, Robert C. Mayer, Theodore J. St. Antoine and Thomas E. Harris for the American Federation of Labor and Congress of Industrial Organizations, and by Bernard M. Mamet for Local 374, International Brotherhood of Boilermakers.

MICHAEL C. SANSONE, Petitioner,

v

UNITED STATES

380 US 343, 13 L ed 2d 882, 85 S Ct 1004

Argued March 10, 1965.   Decided March 29, 1965.

Decision: Defendant indicted for income tax evasion in violation of § 7201 of 1954 Internal Revenue Code held not entitled to instructions concerning lesser-included offenses prohibited by §§ 7203 and 7207.

SUMMARY

The defendant was indicted for violation of § 7201 of the 1954 Internal Revenue Code, declaring it a felony to wilfully attempt to evade federal taxes. He had failed to report in an income tax return a gain from the sale of certain land and had understated his tax liability, but he contended that the understatement was not wilful. At the conclusion of the trial, the defendant requested that the jury be instructed that they could acquit him of violating § 7201, but still convict him of either or both of the asserted lesser-included misdemeanor offenses of wilfully filing a fraudulent or false return, in violation of § 7207, or wilfully failing to pay his taxes when due, in violation of § 7203. The instructions requested by the defendant were denied, the jury found him guilty of violating § 7201, and he received a sentence more severe than would have been permissible for a violation of either § 7203 or § 7207. The conviction was upheld by the Court of Appeals for the Eighth Circuit. (334 F2d 287.)

On certiorari, the United States Supreme Court affirmed. In an opinion by **Goldberg, J.**, expressing the views of seven members of the Court, it was held that since there were no disputed issues of fact which would justify instructing the jury that it could find that the defendant had committed all the elements of either or both of the §§ 7203 and 7207 misdemeanors without having committed a § 7201 felony, the defendant was not entitled to a lesser-included offense charge.

Black and **Douglas, JJ.,** dissented on the ground that there was sufficient evidence to require the granting of the defendant's requested instructions as to the lesser-included offenses.

COUNSEL

Merle L. Silverstein argued the cause for petitioner. With him on the briefs was Stanley M. Rosenblum.

Paul Bender, by special leave of Court, argued the cause for the United States pro hac vice. With him on the brief were Solicitor General Cox, Assistant Attorney General Oberdorfer and Joseph M. Howard.

HENRY

v

COLLINS

HENRY

v

PEARSON

380 US 356, 13 L ed 2d 892, 85 S Ct 992

[Nos. 89 and 90]

March 29, 1965

Decision: State trial court held to have erred in public officials' libel suit by instructing jury that officials could recover upon showing of intent to inflict harm, rather than intent to inflict harm through falsehood.

SUMMARY

A county attorney and a city police chief brought libel suits in the Circuit Court of Coahoma County, Mississippi, against one who stated that his arrest was "the result of a diabolical plot" in which they were implicated. The trial court instructed the jury that it could infer malice from the falsity and libelous nature of the statement. The jury returned verdicts against the defendant, and the Supreme Court of Mississippi affirmed. (— Miss —, 158 So 2d 28; — Miss —, 158 So 2d 695.)

On certiorari, the Supreme Court of the United States reversed. In a per curiam opinion expressing the views of six members of the Court, it was held that the freedom of speech and press prohibits a public official from recovering damages for a defamatory falsehood unless he proves that the statement was made with knowledge that it was false or with reckless disregard of whether or not it was false.

Black, Douglas, and **Goldberg, JJ.,** concurred on the additional ground that it would violate the First and Fourteenth Amendments to subject the defendant to any libel judgment solely because of his criticism of the performance of the plaintiffs' public duties.

COUNSEL

Robert L. Carter, Barbara A. Morris, Jack H. Young and Frank D. Reeves for petitioner in both cases.

W. O. Luckett for respondents in both cases.

O'KEEFFE, Deputy Commissioner,

v

SMITH, HINCHMAN & GRYLLS ASSOCIATES,
Inc., et al.

380 US 359, 13 L ed 2d 895, 85 S Ct 1012

March 29, 1965

Decision: Deputy workmen's compensation commissioner's finding that drowning of private employee on South Korean lake during Saturday outing arose out of and in the course of his employment held improperly reversed.

SUMMARY

A private engineering concern's employee, hired to work in South Korea on a 365-day basis and given a per diem allowance for each day in the year, was drowned while boating on a South Korean lake. A deputy workmen's compensation commissioner determined that the employee's death arose out of and in the course of his employment so as to entitle his widow and minor child to death benefits in accordance with the Longshoremen's and Harbor Workers' Compensation Act, as extended by the Defense Bases Act. The United States District Court for the Middle District of Florida affirmed (222 F Supp 4) but the United States Court of Appeals for the Fifth Circuit reversed (327 F2d 1003).

On certiorari, the Supreme Court of the United States reversed. In a per curiam opinion expressing the views of five members of the Court, it was held that the deputy commissioner's determination should have been affirmed because it was not irrational or without substantial evidence on the record as a whole.

Harlan, J., joined by Clark and White, JJ., dissented on the ground that the employee's death did not arise out of the course of his employment.

Douglas, J., dubitante, stated that the review of the deputy commissioner's findings rested with the Court of Appeals, which he would not be inclined to reverse.

COUNSEL

Solicitor General Cox, Assistant Attorney General Douglas and Morton Hollander for petitioner.
George W. Ericksen for respondents.

FEDERAL TRADE COMMISSION, Petitioner,

v

COLGATE-PALMOLIVE CO. et al.

380 US 374, 13 L ed 2d 904, 85 S Ct 1035

[No. 62]

Argued December 10, 1964. Decided
April 5, 1965.

Decision: Undisclosed use of sand-covered plexiglass in television commercial as "sandpaper" demonstrating moisturizing quality of advertised shaving cream held material deceptive practice forbidden by § 5 of Federal Trade Commission Act.

SUMMARY

In three one-minute television commercials prepared by an advertising agency for a shaving-cream manufacturer, plexiglass to which sand had been applied was shaved clean after the shaving cream was applied, while the announcer informed viewers that to prove the shaving cream's moisturizing power, "this tough, dry sandpaper" would be shaved "in a stroke." The Federal Trade Commission found the commercials to constitute deceptive practices forbidden by § 5 of the Federal Trade Commission Act, and ordered the manufacturer and the agency to cease and desist from presenting a test, experiment, or demonstration that was represented to the public as actual proof of a product claim but was not a genuine test, because of the undisclosed use of a mockup or prop instead of the product or substance represented to be used therein. The United States Court of Appeals for the First Circuit refused to enforce the order. (326 F2d 517.)

[Supreme Ct Sum]

On certiorari, the Supreme Court of the United States reversed. In an opinion by **Warren,** Ch. J., expressing the views of seven members of the Court, it was held that the undisclosed use of plexiglass in the commercials was a material deceptive practice and that the Commission's order was not incapable of practical interpretation as forbidding the use of props in commercials for purposes other than the proof of product claims.

Harlan, J., joined by **Stewart,** J., dissented in part on the ground that the commercials produced on the screen an accurate reproduction of what the viewer would see if the experiment were performed before him with sandpaper.

COUNSEL

Philip B. Heymann argued the cause for petitioner. With him on the briefs were Solicitor General Cox, Assistant Attorney General Orrick and James McI. Henderson.

John F. Sonnett argued the cause for respondents. With him on the brief for Colgate-Palmolive Co. was Arthur Mermin. On the brief for Ted Bates & Co., Inc., were H. Thomas Austern and William H. Allen.

Briefs of amici curiae, urging affirmance, were filed by Mahlon F. Perkins, Jr., for the American Association of Advertising Agencies, Inc., and by Gilbert H. Weil for the Association of National Advertisers, Inc.

BOB GRANVILLE POINTER, Petitioner,

v

STATE OF TEXAS

380 US 400, 13 L ed 2d 923, 85 S Ct 1065

Argued March 15, 1965.   Decided April 5, 1965.

Decision: Right of confrontation, guaranteed by Sixth Amendment, held applicable in state criminal proceedings.

SUMMARY

At the defendant's trial in a Texas state court on a charge of robbery, the state, over defendant's objections, introduced the transcript of a witness' testimony given at the preliminary hearing, at which defendant was not represented by counsel and had no opportunity to cross-examine the witness. The state showed that the witness had moved from Texas with no intention to return. Defendant was convicted and his conviction was affirmed by the Texas Court of Criminal Appeals. (375 SW2d 293.)

On certiorari, the Supreme Court of the United States reversed. In an opinion by **Black, J.,** expressing the views of seven members of the Court, it was held that (1) the Sixth Amendment's guaranty protecting an accused's right to confront the witnesses against him was made obligatory on the states by the Fourteenth Amendment, and (2) the facts, as stated above, constituted a denial of defendant's constitutional right of confrontation.

Harlan and **Stewart,** JJ., in separate opinions, concurred in the result, but dissented from the ruling under (1), supra. **Harlan,** J., voted for reversal on the ground that the right of confrontation is implicit in the concept of ordered liberty reflected in the due process clause of the Fourteenth Amendment independently of the Sixth. Stewart, J., voted for reversal on the ground that defendant was denied the opportunity to cross-examine, through counsel, the chief witness for the prosecution.

Goldberg, J., in a separate concurring opinion, joined in the Court's opinion, specifically stating that he adhered to and supported the process of absorption by means of which the Court held that certain fundamental guaranties of the Bill of Rights are made obligatory on the states through the Fourteenth Amendment.

COUNSEL

Orville A. Harlan, by appointment of the Court, 379 US 911, argued the cause and filed a brief for petitioner.

Gilbert J. Pena, Assistant Attorney General of Texas, argued the cause for respondent. With him on the brief were Waggoner Carr, Attorney General of Texas, Hawthorne Phillips, First Assistant Attorney General, Stanton Stone, Executive Assistant Attorney General, and Howard M. Fender and Allo B. Crow, Jr., Assistant Attorneys General.

JESSE ELLIOTT DOUGLAS, Petitioner,

v

STATE OF ALABAMA

380 US 415, 13 L ed 2d 934, 85 S Ct 1074

Argued March 9 and 10, 1965.

Decided April 5, 1965.

Decision: Accused's constitutional right to confrontation held violated by state prosecutor's reading confession of accomplice who invoked privilege against self-incrimination.

SUMMARY

Defendant was indicted in the Circuit Court of Dallas County, Alabama, on a charge of assault with intent to murder. An accomplice was found guilty in a previous separate trial and, when called as a witness in defendant's trial, invoked his privilege against self-incrimination. Thereupon, the state's attorney produced a confession signed by the accomplice and, in the guise of cross-examination to refresh the witness' recollection, purported to read from the document, the codefendant after every few sentences refusing to answer the attorney's question whether he made the statement embodied in these sentences. Finally the state's attorney called law enforcement officers who identified the document as the accomplice's confession, but the document was not offered in evidence. Defendant's counsel objected three times to the reading of the confession before the jury, but did not renew this objection thereafter, but moved to exclude the confession, and for a mistrial and for a new trial. Defendant was convicted and his conviction was affirmed by the Alabama Court of Appeals. (— Ala App —,

163 So 2d 477.) The Supreme Court of Alabama denied review. (276 Ala 703, 163 So 2d 496.)

On certiorari, the Supreme Court of the United States reversed. In an opinion by Brennan, J., expressing the views of seven members of the Court, it was held that (1) the confrontation clause of the Sixth Amendment is applicable to the states, (2) the facts as stated above constituted a denial of the accused's constitutional right of confrontation, and (3) defendant's counsel had not waived the right to confrontation through failure to make sufficient objection to the reading of the accomplice's confession.

Harlan and Stewart, JJ., in separate concurring opinions, disagreed with the ruling stated under (1), but concurred in the judgment of reversal, on the ground that the defendant was deprived of due process in violation of the Fourteenth Amendment.

COUNSEL

Charles Cleveland argued the cause for petitioner. With him on the brief were Bryan A. Chancey and Robert S. Gordon.

Paul T. Gish, Jr., Assistant Attorney General of Alabama, argued the cause for respondent. With him on the brief was Richmond M. Flowers, Attorney General of Alabama.

OTTO V. BURNETT, Petitioner,

v

NEW YORK CENTRAL RAILROAD COMPANY

380 US 442, 13 L ed 2d 941, 85 S Ct 1050

Argued March 11, 1965.

Decided April 5, 1965.

Decision: Limitation period of Federal Employers' Liability Act held tolled by state court action under the Act, notwithstanding its dismissal for lack of venue.

SUMMARY

Eight days after plaintiff's action under the Federal Employers' Liability Act had been dismissed by an Ohio state court for lack of proper venue, the plaintiff commenced a like action in the United States District Court for the Southern District of Ohio. The District Court dismissed the complaint on the ground that although the state suit was brought within the 3-year limitation period provided in § 6 of the Act, the federal action was not timely. The Court of Appeals for the Sixth Circuit affirmed. (332 F2d 529.)

On certiorari, the United States Supreme Court reversed. In an opinion by Goldberg, J., expressing the views of seven members of the Court, it was held that (1) the timely commencement of the state court action tolled the federal statute of limitations, and (2) the federal limitation provision was tolled until the state court order dismissing the state action became final by the running of the time during which an appeal may be taken or the entry of a final judgment on appeal.

Douglas, J., joined by Black, J., concurred, but found it not necessary to rely on the fact that the federal court action was filed before the time for appealing from the state court dismissal of the former action had expired.

COUNSEL

Douglas G. Cole argued the cause for petitioner. With him on the brief was Otto F. Putnick.

Roy W. Short argued the cause and filed a brief for respondent.

———————

NATIONAL LABOR RELATIONS BOARD,
Petitioner,

v

METROPOLITAN LIFE INSURANCE COMPANY

380 US 438, 13 L ed 2d 951, 85 S Ct 1061

Argued January 21, 1965.
Decided April 5, 1965.

Decision: Extent of unionization held one, though not
the controlling, factor in determining appropriate
bargaining unit.

SUMMARY

On petition of a union, and over the protest of the
employer, an insurance company, as to the appropriateness of the bargaining unit, the National Labor Relations
Board certified the union as the bargaining representative of all debit insurance agents, including all can-
vassing regular and office account agents, at a district
office of the insurer. After the insurer deliberately refused to bargain with the union in order to challenge
the appropriateness of the bargaining unit, the union filed
unfair labor practice charges with the Board, which, ad-
hering to its prior unit determination, held that the
insurer had committed unfair labor practices and ordered
the insurer to bargain with the union (142 NLRB 491).
The Court of Appeals for the First Circuit refused to
enforce this order, on the ground that the Board, in
violation of § 9(c)(5) of the amended National Labor
Relations Act, had regarded the extent of union organization as controlling in determining the appropriate bargaining unit (327 F2d 906).

On certiorari, the United States Supreme Court vacated the judgment of the Court of Appeals and ordered

the case remanded to the National Labor Relations Board for further proceedings. In an opinion by **Goldberg, J.,** expressing the views of eight members of the Court, it was held that the conclusion that the Board had violated § 9(c)(5) was not the only possible one, but that the Board's failure to articulate reasons for its decision rendered judicial review of the decision inappropriate and necessitated further proceedings by the Board.

Douglas, J., dissented on the ground that the Board's order should have been set aside, without the case being remanded for further proceedings.

COUNSEL

Daniel M. Friedman argued the cause for petitioner. On the briefs were Solicitor General Cox, Arnold Ordman, Dominick L. Manoli, Norton J. Come and Warren M. Davison.

Burton A. Zorn argued the cause for respondent. With him on the brief were George G. Gallantz, Thomas F. Delaney and Marvin Dicker.

MELVIN C. JENKINS, Petitioner,

v

UNITED STATES

380 US 445, 13 L ed 2d 957, 85 S Ct 957

Argued April 1, 1965.
Decided April 5, 1965.

Decision: Trial judge's statement that jury must reach verdict in federal criminal prosecution held to have had coercive effect so as to require new trial.

SUMMARY

In defendant's trial in the United States District Court for the District of Columbia on charges of robbery and assault with intent to rob, the jury sent a note to the trial judge advising him that it was unable to reach a verdict "because of insufficient evidence." The judge recalled the jury to the courtroom and in the course of his response stated: "You have got to reach a decision in this case." The jury subsequently found the defendant guilty of robbery. The Court of Appeals for the District of Columbia Circuit affirmed the conviction (117 App DC 346, 330 F2d 220), and a petition for rehearing en banc was denied, four judges dissenting.

On certiorari, the United States Supreme Court reversed and remanded the case for a new trial. In a per curiam opinion expressing the view of seven members of the Court, it was held that in its context and under all the circumstances, the judge's statement to the jury was coercive.

Clark and **Harlan, JJ.,** dissented without opinion.

COUNSEL

H. Thomas Sisk argued the cause for petitioner. With him on the brief were M. Michael Cramer and David B. Isbell.

Philip B. Heymann argued the cause for the United States. On the brief were Solicitor General Cox, Assistant Attorney General Miller and Philip R. Monahan.

AMERICAN OIL COMPANY, Appellant,

v

P. G. NEILL et al.

380 US 451, 14 L ed 2d 1, 85 S Ct 1130

Argued January 25 and 26, 1965.

Decided April 26, 1965.

Decision: State excise tax held violative of due process clause as applied to sale occurring outside state.

SUMMARY

An oil company which was incorporated in Delaware and was licensed in Idaho as a dealer in motor fuels sold a quantity of gasoline to the federal government for the use of a federal agency located in Idaho. The invitation, submission, and acceptance of bids for the contract of sale occurred outside of Idaho, and although the federal government arranged for the gasoline to be brought from the place of delivery into Idaho, delivery was effected outside of Idaho. Under Idaho statutes, an excise tax of 6 cents per gallon was imposed on all motor fuels "received" by a licensed Idaho dealer, and "motor fuel which is in any manner supplied, sold or furnished to any person or agency, whatsoever, not the holder of an uncanceled Idaho dealer permit, by an Idaho licensed dealer, for importation into the state of Idaho from a point of origin outside the state, shall be considered to be received by the Idaho licensed dealer so supplying, selling or furnishing such motor fuel, immediately after the imported motor fuel has been unloaded in the state of Idaho." After paying this tax under protest, the oil company sued in an Idaho state court for a refund. The company was granted summary judgment by the trial judge on the ground that the imposition of the tax violated the due process and commerce clauses of the Federal Constitution, but the Idaho Supreme Court reversed, holding the constitutional objections to be without merit. (86 Idaho 7, 383 P2d 350.)

On appeal, the United States Supreme Court reversed and remanded the case, holding that the imposition of the tax violated the due process clause. In an opinion by Warren, Ch. J., expressing the views of eight members of the Court, it was held that controlling effect must be given to the finding that the incidence of the excise tax fell on the dealer, that is, the oil company; that every phase of the sale occurred outside of Idaho and was entirely unconnected with the company's business in Idaho; and that the fact that the company sold the gasoline with knowledge that it would be imported into and used within Idaho, and the fact that the company had been authorized to do business in Idaho as a dealer in motor fuels, were insufficient considerations to uphold the tax as against attack under the due process clause.

Black, J., dissented without opinion.

COUNSEL

Frank I. Goodman argued the cause for appellant. Allan G. Shepard argued the cause for appellees.

EDDIE V. HANNA, Petitioner,

v

EDWARD M. PLUMER, Jr., Executor

380 US 460, 14 L ed 2d 8, 85 S Ct 1136

Argued January 21, 1965.

Decided April 26, 1965.

Decision: Federal Civil Procedure Rule 4(d)(1), authorizing service of process upon an individual by leaving copies of summons and complaint at his usual place of abode, rather than state law requiring "delivery in hand," held applicable in diversity action.

SUMMARY

The plaintiff, a citizen of Ohio, filed her complaint in the United States District Court for the District of Massachusetts to recover for personal injuries resulting from an automobile accident allegedly caused by the negligence of a Massachusetts citizen deceased at the time of the filing of the complaint. Service was made upon the executor of the deceased by leaving, in compliance with Federal Civil Procedure Rule 4(d)(1), copies of the summons and the complaint with the executor's wife at his residence. Because Massachusetts law required service by "delivery in hand" upon the executor, the District Court entered summary judgment for defendant, and the Court of Appeals for the First Circuit affirmed. (331 F2d 157.)

On certiorari, the United States Supreme Court reversed. In an opinion by Warren, Ch. J., expressing the views of eight members of the Court, it was held that Rule 4(d)(1) transgressed neither constitutional bounds nor exceeded the congressional mandate embodied in the Rules Enabling Act, which provides that the rules pre-

scribed by the Supreme Court for the practice and procedure of the federal district courts in civil actions shall
not abridge, enlarge, or modify "any substantive right."
It was further held that the Rule was the standard against
which the District Court should have measured the ade-
quacy of the service.

Harlan, J., concurred in the result, but expressed the
view that the Court misconceived the constitutional prem-
ises of Erie R. Co. v Tompkins and failed to deal ade-
quately with those past decisions upon which the courts
below relied.

COUNSEL

Albert P. Zabin argued the cause for petitioner, pro
hac vice, by special leave of Court.

James J. Fitzpatrick argued the cause for respondent.

JAMES A. DOMBROWSKI et al., Appellants,

v

JAMES H. PFISTER, etc., et al.

380 US 479, 14 L ed 2d 22, 85 S Ct 1116

Argued January 25, 1965.

Decided April 26, 1965.

Decision: Federal injunctive relief against criminal prosecution threatened under Louisiana subversive activities statute to discourage plaintiffs from continuing their civil rights activities held proper without awaiting state court interpretation of statute; statute held invalid.

SUMMARY

The plaintiffs, an organization and individuals active in fostering civil rights for Negroes in Louisiana, filed a complaint in the United States District Court for the Eastern District of Louisiana, seeking declaratory relief and an injunction restraining defendants from prosecuting or threatening to prosecute plaintiffs for alleged violations of the Louisiana Subversive Activities and Communist Control Law and the Louisiana Communist Propaganda Control Law. The complaint alleged that the statutes were invalid on their face and that the threats to enforce them against the plaintiffs were made only to discourage them from continuing their civil rights activities. A three-judge District Court dismissed the complaint for failure to state a claim upon which relief could be granted. (227 F Supp 556.)

On appeal, the United States Supreme Court reversed. In an opinion by Brennan, J., expressing the views of five members of the Court, it was held that (1) the complaint alleged sufficient irreparable injury to justify equitable relief, (2) it was improper for the District Court to abstain from a decision pending authoritative state court interpretation of the statutes, since the abstention doctrine is inapplicable in cases in which statutes are justifiably attacked on their face as abridging free expression or as applied for the purpose of discouraging protected activities, (3) the statute making it a felony to participate in the formation or management or to contribute to the support of "any subversive organization," as defined in the statute, was invalid on the ground of vagueness, and (4) the statute creating an offense of failure to register as a member of a Communist-front organization was invalid because containing an invalid presumption as to the status of the organizations affected by the statute.

Harlan and Clark, JJ., dissented on the Court's holding under (2), supra, expressing the view that the District Court should have retained jurisdiction for the purpose of affording plaintiffs appropriate relief in the event that the state prosecution did not go forward in a prompt and bona fide manner.

Black and Stewart, JJ., did not participate.

COUNSEL

Leon Hubert and Arthur Kinoy argued the cause for appellants.

John E. Jackson, Jr. and Jack N. Rogers for appellees.

AMERICAN COMMITTEE FOR PROTECTION
OF FOREIGN BORN, Petitioner,

v

SUBVERSIVE ACTIVITIES CONTROL BOARD

380 US 503, 14 L ed 2d 39, 85 S Ct 1148

Argued December 8 and 9, 1964.
Decided April 26, 1965.

Decision: Judgment affirming order requiring organization to register as Communist-front organization
vacated to bring record up to date since death of
organization's executive director whose activities
were substantial basis for order.

SUMMARY

Based primarily on evidence taken at a hearing concluded in 1955, which tended to prove that an organization's executive director was a Communist Party member, the Subversive Activities Control Board ordered in
1960 that the organization register as a "Communist-
front" organization under § 7 of the Subversive Activities
Control Act, although the executive director had died in
1959 and the record disclosed no evidence of the organization's activities after his death. The United States
Court of Appeals for the District of Columbia Circuit
affirmed. (117 App DC 393, 331 F2d 53.)

On certiorari, the Supreme Court of the United States
vacated the Court of Appeals' judgment. In a per curiam opinion expressing the views of five members of
the Court, it was held that since the order operated
prospectively, the record should be brought up to date
to take account of supervening events.

Black, J., dissenting, stated that the Subversive Activities Control Act is unconstitutional.

Douglas, J., joined by **Black** and **Harlan, JJ.**, dissented on the ground that the case was alive and unaffected by the executive director's death.

White, J., did not participate.

COUNSEL

Joseph Forer argued the cause for petitioner. Bruce J. Terris argued the cause for respondent.

VETERANS OF THE ABRAHAM LINCOLN
BRIGADE, Petitioner,

v

SUBVERSIVE ACTIVITIES CONTROL BOARD

380 US 513, 14 L ed 2d 46, 85 S Ct 1153

Argued December 9, 1964.
Decided April 26, 1965.

Decision: Judgment affirming Subversive Activities Control Board order directing organization to register as Communist-front organization vacated where order was entered on stale record.

SUMMARY

Based almost exclusively on events before 1950, and very largely on events before 1940, the Subversive Activities Control Board ordered an organization to register as a Communist-front organization under § 7 of the Subversive Activities Control Act. The United States Court of Appeals for the District of Columbia Circuit affirmed. (117 US App DC 404, 331 F2d 64.)

On certiorari, the Supreme Court of the United States vacated the judgment. In a per curiam opinion expressing the views of five members of the Court, it was held that the record was too stale for the decision of the serious constitutional questions raised by the order.

Black, J., dissenting, stated that the Subversive Activities Control Act is unconstitutional.

Douglas, J., joined by **Black** and **Harlan, JJ.,** dissented on the ground that the case was ripe for decision.

White, J., did not participate.

COUNSEL

Leonard B. Boudin argued the cause for petitioner.
Kevin T. Maroney and Bruce J. Terris argued the
cause for respondent.

A. M. HARMAN, Jr., et al., Appellants,

v

LARS FORSSENIUS et al.

380 US 528, 14 L ed 2d 50, 85 S Ct 1177

Argued March 1 and 2, 1965.

Decided April 27, 1965.

Decision: Virginia statute requiring, as a prerequisite to voting in federal elections, either payment of poll tax or filing of certificate of residence, held invalid as violating the Twenty-Fourth Amendment.

SUMMARY

Two class actions were filed in the United States District Court for the Eastern District of Virginia, attacking the validity of a Virginia statute which required, in order to qualify to vote in federal elections, either payment of a poll tax or the filing of a certificate of residence. The District Court entered judgments for the plaintiffs. (235 F Supp 66.)

On appeal, the United States Supreme Court affirmed. In an opinion by **Warren, Ch. J.,** expressing the views of eight members of the Court, it was held that (1) the statute violated the Twenty-Fourth Amendment, providing that the right of citizens of the United States to vote in any federal election shall not be denied or abridged by reason of failure to pay any poll tax, and (2) the District Court properly refused to stay the proceedings until the Virginia state courts had been afforded a reasonable opportunity to pass on underlying issues of state law and to construe the statutes involved.

Harlan, J., agreed with the Court's opinion insofar as it rested on the proposition that the Twenty-Fourth

Amendment forbids the use of a state poll tax for any purpose whatever in determining voter qualifications in all elections for federal office, and also agreed that this was not a case for application of the abstention doctrine.

COUNSEL

Joseph C. Carter, Jr., argued the cause for appellants. H. E. Widener, Jr., argued the cause for appellees.

Harold H. Greene argued the cause for the United States, amicus curiae, by special leave of Court.

R. WRIGHT ARMSTRONG, Jr., Petitioner,

v

SALVATORE E. MANZO et ux.

380 US 545, 14 L ed 2d 62, 85 S Ct 1187

Argued on March 9, 1965.

Decided on April 27, 1965.

Decision: Due process held violated by failure to give divorced father notice of pending proceeding for adoption of his child.

SUMMARY

In proceedings instituted in the District Court of El Paso County, Texas, by a divorced mother and her new husband for the adoption of a child from the mother's first marriage, no notice of the pendency of the proceedings was given to the divorced father of the child, although the parties initiating the adoption proceedings well knew his precise whereabouts in Texas. After the adoption decree was entered, the father was notified of the adoption and promptly filed a motion to set aside the decree and grant a new trial. The District Court, without setting aside the adoption decree, granted a hearing on the motion, which was denied. The appropriate Texas Court of Civil Appeals affirmed (371 SW 2d 407) and the Supreme Court of Texas refused an application for writ of error.

On certiorari, the Supreme Court of the United States reversed. In an opinion by Stewart, J., expressing the unanimous views of the Court, it was held that (1) the failure to notify the divorced father of the pendent adoption proceedings deprived him of due process of law and rendered the decree constitutionally invalid, and (2) the subsequent hearing did not cure its constitutional invalidity.

COUNSEL

Ewell Lee Smith, Jr., argued the cause for petitioner. William Duncan argued the cause for respondents.

GENERAL MOTORS CORPORATION, Petitioner,

v

DISTRICT OF COLUMBIA

380 US 553, 14 L ed 2d 68, 85 S Ct 1156

Argued March 10, 1965.

Decided April 27, 1965.

Decision: Regulation of tax commissioners basing apportionment formula for determining income of corporation subject to local franchise tax exclusively upon sales factor held unauthorized under District of Columbia Income and Franchise Tax Act.

SUMMARY

The District of Columbia Income and Franchise Tax Act, providing that the measure of the franchise tax imposed by the statute shall be that portion of the net income of a corporation as is fairly attributable to the trade or business carried on by it within the District and that the net income of a business carried on both within and without the District shall be deemed to be from sources within and without the District, in a separate provision authorized the District Tax Commissioners to prescribe the methods of determining the portion of income attributable to the District. In the exercise of this authority the District Tax Commissioners promulgated a regulation to the effect that the portion of the income to be apportioned to the District shall be such percentage of the total income of a corporation as the District sales bear to the total sales of the corporation everywhere.

The Court of Appeals for the District of Columbia in an en banc decision approved the application of the above regulation in determining, for the purpose of computing the franchise tax due, the proportion of the total net income allocated to the District of an automobile manufacturer which made substantial sales to customers within the District, but which carried on no manufacturing operations there. (336 F2d 885.)

On certiorari, the United States Supreme Court reversed. In an opinion by **Stewart, J.**, expressing the views of seven members of the Court, it was held that the regulation was not authorized by the statute, since the statutory language does not permit the application of an apportionment formula which makes use of the sales factor alone to the exclusion of other factors such as geographical distribution of the corporation's payroll and property.

Black, J., and **Douglas, J.**, dissented on the ground that the tax was authorized by the controlling statute.

COUNSEL

Donald K. Barnes argued the cause for petitioner.
Henry E. Wixon argued the cause for respondent.

COMMISSIONER OF INTERNAL REVENUE,
Petitioner,

v

CLAY B. BROWN et al.

380 US 563, 14 L ed 2d 75, 85 S Ct 1162

Argued March 3, 1965.
Decided April 27, 1965.

Decision: Transfer of business to tax-exempt foundation held to be "sale" for income tax purposes and entitled to capital gains treatment, although purchase price was payable in instalments out of future operating profits of business and business was leased to newly formed corporation.

SUMMARY

After being approached by a tax-exempt institute and after considerable negotiation, the taxpayers, who were stockholders of a lumber company, agreed to sell their stock to the institute for $1,300,000, payable $5,000 down from the assets of the company and the balance within 10 years from the earnings of the company's assets. It was provided that simultaneously with the transfer of the stock the institute would liquidate the company and lease its assets for 5 years to a new corporation formed and wholly owned by the attorneys for the taxpayers. The new corporation was to pay to the institute 80 percent of its operating profit without allowance for depreciation or taxes, and 90 percent of such payments were to be paid by the institute to the taxpayers to apply on the $1,300,000 note. The note was noninterest-bearing, the institute had no obligation to pay it except from the rental income, and it was secured by mortgages and assignments of the assets transferred or leased to the new corporation.

If the payments on the note failed to total $250,000 over any 2 consecutive years, the taxpayers could declare the entire balance of the note due and payable. None of the taxpayers became stockholders or directors of the new corporation, but it was provided that the president of the taxpayers' company was to have a management contract with the new corporation at an annual salary and the right to name any successor manager if he resigned. When the transaction was closed, the new corporation immediately took over operations of the business under its lease, on the same premises and with practically the same personnel as had been employed previously. Effective several months later, the president of the taxpayers' company resigned as general manager of the new corporation and waived his right to name a successor. Two or three years thereafter, because of a rapidly declining lumber market, the new corporation suffered severe reverses and its operations were terminated. The taxpayers did not repossess the property under their mortgages, but agreed that they should be sold by the institute and that the institute would retain 10 percent of the proceeds. Accordingly, the property was sold by the institute for $300,000. The payments on the note from rentals and from the sale of the properties totaled over $900,000, which was recorded by the taxpayers as a long-term capital gain. However, the Commissioner of Internal Revenue instituted proceedings in the United States Tax Court, contending that the taxpayers' transaction with the institute was not a bona fide sale and was not entitled to long-term capital gains treatment. The Tax Court, rejecting these contentions, decided in favor of the taxpayers (37 T Ct 461), and the Court of Appeals for the Ninth Circuit affirmed (325 F2d 313).

On certiorari, the United States Supreme Court affirmed. In an opinion by White, J., expressing the views of five members of the Court, it was held that for tax purposes, the transaction was a "sale" and was entitled to long-term capital gains treatment.

Harlan, J., concurring in the result, stated that the position taken by the Commissioner was unsound, but that the case might have been different if the Commissioner had argued that (1) the only interest which the stockholders exchanged was their interest in the ability of the business to produce income in excess of that which was necessary to pay them off under the terms of the transaction, and (2) the stockholders should have received capital gains treatment only to the extent of such an exchange.

Goldberg, J., joined by Warren, Ch. J., and Black, J., dissented on the ground that the transaction was an "artful device" for avoiding taxes and did not involve a sufficient shift of economic risk or control of the business to warrant being treated as a "sale" for tax purposes.

COUNSEL

Wayne G. Barnett argued the cause for petitioner.
William H. Kinsey argued the cause for respondents.

FEDERAL TRADE COMMISSION, Petitioner,

v

CONSOLIDATED FOODS CORPORATION

380 US 592, 14 L ed 2d 95, 85 S Ct 1220

Argued March 10 and 11, 1965.

Decided April 28, 1965.

Decision: Acquisition by large food concern of company commanding a substantial share of the dehydrated onion and garlic market held to violate § 7 of the Clayton Act.

SUMMARY

A company engaged in the manufacture and sale of food acquired a corporation manufacturing dehydrated onion and garlic whose sales accounted for about one-third of the total industry sales, and if combined with those of its principal competitor, for about 90 percent of such sales. The Federal Trade Commission held that the acquisition violated § 7 of the Clayton Act on the ground that such acquisition might result in a substantial lessening of competition, and accordingly ordered divestiture. The Court of Appeals for the Seventh Circuit, relying mainly on 10 years of postacquisition experience, set the order of the Federal Trade Commission aside, holding that the Commission had failed to show a probability that the acquisition would substantially lessen competition. (329 F2d 623.)

On certiorari, the Supreme Court of the United States reversed. In an opinion by **Douglas, J.**, expressing the view of seven members of the Court, it was held that there was substantial evidence to sustain the conclusion of the commission that since the acquisition was of a company commanding a substantial share of the market, the probability of reciprocal buying existed and new entry by other companies was discouraged.

Stewart, J., concurring, agreed with the result stated, but differed with the Court in its assessment of the weight to be accorded postacquisition evidence.

Harlan, J., concurring, agreed with the views as expressed by Stewart, J., with the exception that he wanted it understood that only evidence could be drawn on upon which the Commission acted.

COUNSEL

Solicitor General Archibald Cox argued the cause for petitioner.

Daniel Walker argued the cause for respondent.

EDDIE DEAN GRIFFIN, Petitioner,

v

STATE OF CALIFORNIA

380 US 609, 14 L ed 2d 106, 85 S Ct 1229

Argued March 9, 1965.
Decided April 28, 1965.

Decision: Comment by counsel and court on accused's failure to testify at state criminal prosecution held constitutionally barred.

SUMMARY

In a prosecution resulting in a murder conviction in the Superior Court of Los Angeles County, California, the failure of the accused to testify was commented upon by the prosecuting attorney and, in its instructions, by the court; both the prosecuting attorney and the court acted pursuant to Article I, § 13 of the California Constitution, which provides that in any criminal case, whether defendant testifies or not, his failure to explain or deny by his testimony any evidence or facts in the case against him may be commented upon by the court, and by counsel, and may be considered by the court or the jury. On appeal from the conviction, the Supreme Court of California affirmed. (60 Cal 2d 182, 32 Cal Rptr 24, 383 P2d 432.)

On certiorari, the Supreme Court of the United States reversed the conviction. In an opinion by **Douglas, J.,** reflecting the views of six members of the Court, it was held that the self-incrimination guaranty of the Fifth Amendment, in its bearing on the states by reason of the Fourteenth Amendment, forbids either comment by the prosecution on an accused's silence or instructions by the court that such silence is evidence of guilt.

Feeling bound by precedent, **Harlan, J.**, concurring, agreed, with reluctance, that the Fifth Amendment bars adverse comment by prosecutors and judges on a defendant's failure to take the stand in a state criminal trial, but reiterated his disagreement with the earlier decisions of the Court that the Fifth Amendment applies to the states in all its refinements.

Stewart, J., joined by **White, J.**, dissented, stating that no violation of the privilege against self-incrimination was involved in the California constitutional provision in question.

COUNSEL

Morris Lavine argued the cause for petitioner.

Albert W. Harris, Jr., argued the cause for respondent.

PARAGON JEWEL COAL COMPANY, Inc.,
Petitioner,

v

COMMISSIONER OF INTERNAL REVENUE

———

COMMISSIONER OF INTERNAL REVENUE,
Petitioner,

v

ROBERT LEE MERRITT et al.

380 US 624, 14 L ed 2d 116, 85 S Ct 1207

Argued March 8, 1965.
Decided April 28, 1965.

Decision: Contract coal miners held not entitled to share depletion deduction under Internal Revenue Code with lessee of coal lands.

SUMMARY

Consolidated tax cases presented the issue whether the lessee of coal lands was entitled to the entire percentage depletion deduction on the gross income from the sale of the coal under the Internal Revenue Code (26 USC §§ 611, 613(b)(4)), or whether contract miners, who had entered into oral agreements with the lessee, had an economic interest in the coal in place, entitling them to share in the depletion allowance. Under the mining agreements between the lessee and the contract miners, the latter were to receive a fixed fee from the lessee for each ton of coal delivered, made investments in equipment rather than in the coal in place, were not obligated to mine the coal to exhaustion, and did not share in the proceeds of the lessee's sale of the coal, and the lessee had the right to change the fee paid to the miners, and to terminate the agreements at will. The Tax Court held that the lessee was entitled to the entire depletion deduction (39 T Ct 257), but the United States Court of Appeals for the Fourth Circuit reversed, holding that the contract miners were entitled to an allocable portion of the deduction (330 F2d 161).

On writs of certiorari, the Supreme Court of the United States reversed the judgments of the Court of Appeals. In an opinion by **Clark, J.**, expressing the views of seven members of the Court, it was held that under the facts of the case the lessee was entitled to the entire depletion deduction, and the contract miners had no economic interest in the coal in place which would entitle them to share in the deduction.

Goldberg, J., joined by **Black, J.**, dissented on the ground that in view of the contract miners' substantial investment in the operation of the mines, they had an economic interest in the coal in place, and were entitled to share in the depletion allowance with the lessee.

COUNSEL

Frederick Bernays Wiener argued the cause for petitioner in the Paragon Jewel Coal Co. Case.

Philip B. Heymann argued the cause for respondent in the Paragon Jewel Coal Co. Case and the petitioner in the Merritt Case.

John Y. Merrell argued the cause for respondents in the Merritt Case.

———————

BROTHERHOOD OF RAILWAY AND STEAM-
SHIP CLERKS, FREIGHT HANDLERS,
EXPRESS AND STATION
EMPLOYEES, Petitioner,

v

ASSOCIATION FOR THE BENEFIT OF
NON-CONTRACT EMPLOYEES
(No. 138)

UNITED AIR LINES, Inc., Petitioner,

v

NATIONAL MEDIATION BOARD et al.
(No. 139)

NATIONAL MEDIATION BOARD et al.,
Petitioners,

v

ASSOCIATION FOR THE BENEFIT OF
NON-CONTRACT EMPLOYEES
(No. 369)

380 US 650, 14 L ed 2d 133, 85 S Ct 1192

Argued March 4, 1965.
Decided April 28, 1965.

Decision: Air carrier held not entitled to be a party to
proceedings by which National Mediation Board
determines the scope of the appropriate bargaining
unit; Board's choice of ballot without space for voting for "no union" held not to exceed its statutory
authority and hence not open for judicial review.

SUMMARY

Over the objection of the employer air carrier, the National Mediation Board, under § 2, Ninth of the Railway Labor Act, ordered an election in the clerical and service employees' unit to determine which of two rival unions, if either, would be the unit's bargaining representative. The carrier then filed an action in the United States District Court for the District of Columbia Circuit, attacking the form of ballot the Board intended to use in the election, because the ballot provided no space for voting for "no union," and contending that the Board should hold a hearing under the statute, with the employer's participation, to determine the appropriate unit in which the election should be held. The case was dismissed and the dismissal was affirmed by the Court of Appeals for the District of Columbia Circuit. (117 App DC 387, 330 F2d 853.) It was before the United States Supreme Court as No. 139. After the dismissal an association for the noncontract employees of the carrier filed a suit against the Board in the same District Court, one of the rival unions being permitted to intervene, and raised substantially the same claims. The District Court enjoined the Board from conducting an election with a ballot that did not permit an employee to cast a vote against collective bargaining representation; the other issues were remanded to the Board for further consideration. (218 F Supp 114.) On appeals by the Board and the intervening union, the Court of Appeals affirmed by a divided court. (117 App DC 387, 330 F2d 853.) These cases are before the United States Supreme Court as Nos. 138 and 369.

On writs of certiorari, the United States Supreme Court reversed the judgments in Nos. 138 and 369, and affirmed the judgment in No. 139. In an opinion by Clark, J., expressing the views of seven members of the

Court, it was held that (1) the Board satisfied its statutory duty to investigate the representation dispute, (2) the employer was not entitled to be a party to proceedings by which the Board determined the scope of the appropriate unit, and in any event was given an adequate role in these proceedings, and (3) the Board's choice of ballot for its future elections did not exceed its statutory authority and was therefore not open to judicial review.

Stewart, J., dissented from the Court's approval of the form of ballot used by the Board in representation elections.

Black, J., concurred in the result, without writing an opinion.

COUNSEL

Solicitor General Archibald Cox argued the cause for respondents in No. 139 and the petitioners in No. 369.

James L. Highsaw, Jr., argued the cause for petitioner in No. 138.

Stuart Bernstein argued the cause for petitioner in No. 139.

Alex L. Arguello argued the cause for respondent in Nos. 138 and 369.

COMMISSIONER OF INTERNAL REVENUE,
Petitioner,

v

ESTATE OF MARSHAL L. NOEL, Deceased,
William H. Frantz and Ruth M.
Noel, Executors

380 US 678, 14 L ed 2d 159, 85 S Ct 1238

Argued April 1, 1965.
Decided April 29, 1965.

Decision: Proceeds of flight insurance held includible, for
federal estate tax purposes, in insured's estate.

SUMMARY

Before boarding an airplane, a husband took out two
round-trip flight insurance policies, naming his wife as
beneficiary. The policy contracts granted the husband
the right either to assign the policies or to change the
beneficiary without his wife's consent. Shortly after the
takeoff, the plane crashed and the husband was killed.
The proceeds of the policies were not included in the
estate tax return filed by his executors. The Commissioner of Internal Revenue determined that the proceeds
of the policies should have been included under 26 USC
§ 2042(2), and the United States Tax Court sustained
that determination. (39 T Ct 466.) The Court of Appeals for the Third Circuit reversed. (332 F2d 950.)

On certiorari, the United States Supreme Court reversed the judgment of the Court of Appeals and affirmed
the judgment of the Tax Court. In an opinion by **Black**,
J., expressing the views of eight members of the Court,
it was held that (1) the flight insurance policies, whether
called "flight accident insurance" or "life insurance," were
in effect insurance taken out on the "life of the decedent"

within the meaning of § 2042(2), and (2) were includible in his gross estate under that statute, since at his death he possessed "incidents of ownership," namely, the right to assign the policies and to change the beneficiary.

Douglas, J., dissented without opinion.

COUNSEL

John B. Jones argued the cause for petitioner.
Harry Norman Ball argued the cause for respondents.

WARREN TRADING POST COMPANY,
Appellant,

v

ARIZONA STATE TAX COMMISSION et al.

380 US 685, 14 L ed 2d 165, 85 S Ct 1242

Argued March 9, 1965.
Decided April 29, 1965.

Decision: Imposition of state tax on trading post company's income from sales to Indians on reservation held invalid on ground of inconsistency with federal statutes.

SUMMARY

The state of Arizona levied a 2 percent tax on a trading post company's gross proceeds of sales, or gross income, derived from a retail trading business with reservation Indians on a Navajo Indian Reservation under a license granted by the United States Indian Commissioner, pursuant to federal statute. Although the company claimed that the tax was invalid on the ground of inconsistency with a comprehensive congressional plan to regulate Indian trade and traders and to have Indian tribes on reservations govern themselves, the Arizona Supreme Court upheld the tax, one justice dissenting. (95 Ariz 110, 387 P2d 809.)

On appeal the United States Supreme Court reversed. In an opinion by **Black, J.,** expressing the unanimous view of the Court, it was held that the tax could not be imposed consistently with federal statutes applicable to the Indians on the reservation.

COUNSEL

Edward Jacobson argued the cause for appellant.
Philip M. Haggerty argued the cause for appellees.

ONE 1958 PLYMOUTH SEDAN, Petitioner,

v

COMMONWEALTH OF PENNSYLVANIA

380 US 693, 14 L ed 2d 170, 85 S Ct 1246

Argued March 31, 1965.
Decided April 29, 1965.

Decision: Constitutional exclusionary rule as to evidence obtained through unreasonable search and seizure held applicable in state proceedings for forfeiture of automobile used for illegal transportation or possession of liquor.

SUMMARY

After two state liquor control board officers, acting without a warrant, stopped and searched an automobile, they found that it contained many cases of liquor not bearing state tax seals. In proceedings instituted by the state for forfeiture of the automobile, the trial judge, concluding that the officers had acted without probable cause, granted a dismissal on the ground that the forfeiture of the automobile depended upon the admission of evidence illegally obtained in violation of the Fourth Amendment to the United States Constitution as applied to the states by the Fourteenth Amendment. However, the Pennsylvania Superior Court, in a 4–3 decision, reversed the order dismissing the proceedings and directed the automobile to be forfeited. (199 Pa Super 428, 186 A2d 52.) The Superior Court's decision was affirmed, with one judge dissenting, by the Pennsylvania Supreme Court, which held that the constitutional rule requiring the evidence to be excluded applied only to criminal prosecutions and not to a forfeiture proceeding, and that it was therefore unnecessary to review the trial judge's finding as to the lack of probable cause. (414 Pa 540, 201 A2d 427.)

On certiorari, the United States Supreme Court reversed and remanded the case. In an opinion by **Goldberg, J.**, expressing the views of eight members of the Court, it was held that the constitutional exclusionary rule was applicable to forfeiture proceedings of the character involved in the instant case, and that, upon remand, the court was free to review the trial judge's finding that the officers acted without probable cause.

Black, J., concurring, stated that the decision should be based upon the Fifth Amendment's protection against self-incrimination as well as upon the Fourth Amendment's protection against unreasonable search and seizure.

COUNSEL

Stanford Shmukler argued the cause for petitioner.

Thomas J. Shannon argued the cause for respondent.

LOUIS ZEMEL, Appellant,

v

DEAN RUSK, Secretary of State, et al.

381 US —, 14 L ed 2d 179, 85 S Ct 1271

Argued March 1, 1965.

Decided May 3, 1965.

Decision: Secretary of State held statutorily authorized to refuse to validate passports of United States citizens for travel to Cuba; the exercise of such authority held constitutionally permissible.

SUMMARY

The Department of State denied a United States citizen's request to have his passport validated for travel to Cuba as a tourist and for the purpose of satisfying his curiosity about the state of affairs in that country. The citizen then instituted a suit against the Secretary of State and the Attorney General in the United States District Court for the District of Connecticut, seeking, among other relief, a judgment declaring that he was entitled under the Constitution and laws of the United States to travel to Cuba and to have his passport validated for that purpose, that the Secretary's restrictions upon travel to Cuba were invalid, and that the Passport Act of 1926 and § 215 of the Immigration and Nationality Act of 1952 were unconstitutional. A three-judge court, by a divided vote, granted the Secretary of State's motion for summary judgment and dismissed the action against the Attorney General. (228 F Supp 65.)

On direct appeal, the United States Supreme Court affirmed. In an opinion by Warren, Ch. J., expressing the views of six members of the Court, it was held that (1) a three-judge court was properly convened, (2) the

Passport Act of 1926 embodies a grant of authority to the Executive to impose area restrictions on the right to travel and to refuse to validate the passports of United States citizens for travel to Cuba, (3) the Secretary's refusal violated neither due process nor the First Amendment's guaranty of free speech, (4) the Passport Act contains sufficiently definite standards for the formulation of travel controls by the Executive, and (5) the court below was correct in refusing to reach the issue of criminal liability under § 215(b) of the Immigration and Nationality Act of 1952.

Black, J., dissented on the ground that the Passport Act violated the provision in Article 1 of the Constitution granting all legislative power to Congress.

Douglas, J., joined by **Goldberg, J.,** dissented, expressing the view that restrictions on the right to travel in times of peace should be so particularized that a First Amendment right is not precluded unless some clear countervailing national interest stands in the way of its assertion.

Goldberg, J., dissented also on the ground that the Executive does not possess inherent power to impose area restrictions on traveling in peacetime, and that Congress has not granted such authority to the Executive.

COUNSEL

Leonard B. Boudin argued the cause for appellant. Solicitor General Archibald Cox argued the cause for appellees.

MARYLAND, for the use of Nadine Y. Levin,
Sydney L. Johns, et al., Petitioners,

v

UNITED STATES

381 US —, 14 L ed 2d 205, 85 S Ct 1293

Argued March 15, 1965.
Decided May 3, 1965.

Decision: Civilian and military member of National
Guard unit which is not in active federal service
held not employee of United States for purposes of
Federal Tort Claims Act.

SUMMARY

As a result of the negligence of the pilot of a jet trainer
assigned to the Maryland Air National Guard, the trainer
collided with a commercial airliner, whose passengers
and crew were killed in the collision, as was a passenger
on the trainer. Two days a month the pilot served as
a commissioned officer in the Guard, which was not in
active federal service, and during the rest of the month
he was employed by the Guard in the civilian capacity
of supervising the maintenance of the squadron aircraft
assigned to the Guard but owned by the United States.
On the day of the collision he had obtained permission
from his superior to take a passenger on a flight in order
to interest the passenger in joining the Guard. Representatives of the estates of the passengers of the airliner
who were victims of the collision filed suit against the
United States under the Federal Tort Claims Act in
the District Court for the Western District of Pennsylvania. Judgment was rendered for the plaintiffs, but
the Court of Appeals for the Third Circuit reversed on

the ground that the pilot of the trainer was not an "employee" of the United States within the meaning of the Federal Tort Claims Act. (329 F2d 722.)

On certiorari, the United States Supreme Court affirmed. In an opinion by **Harlan, J.**, expressing the views of eight members of the Court, liability of the United States under the Federal Tort Claims Act was denied on the ground that in both his military and his civilian capacity the pilot of the trainer was an employee of the state of Maryland and not of the United States.

Douglas, J., dissented without opinion.

COUNSEL

Theodore E. Wolcott argued the cause for petitioners. David Rose argued the cause for respondent.

UNITED STATES, Petitioner,

v

MIDLAND-ROSS CORPORATION

381 US —, 14 L ed 2d 214, 85 S Ct 1308

Argued March 31, 1965.
Decided May 3, 1965.

Decision: Gain from sale of discounted, noninterest-bearing promissory notes held taxable under Internal Revenue Code of 1939 as ordinary income, rather than as capital gain.

SUMMARY

The issue presented in a tax refund case was whether, under the Internal Revenue Code of 1939, the gains realized by the taxpayer from his sale of noninterest-bearing promissory notes, which he had purchased from the issuers at prices discounted below the face amounts, were taxable as capital gains, as contended by the taxpayer, or as ordinary income, as asserted by the Commissioner of Internal Revenue. The taxpayer had sold the notes before maturity for less than their face amounts but more than their issue prices, and the taxpayer's gain from such sales was the economic equivalent of interest for the use of the money to the date of sale. The District Court for the Northern District of Ohio found in favor of the taxpayer (214 F Supp 631), and the Court of Appeals for the Sixth Circuit affirmed (335 F2d 561).

On certiorari, the Supreme Court of the United States reversed. In an opinion by Brennan, J., expressing the unanimous view of the Court, it was held that the earned original issue discount on the notes, which served the same function as stated interest, was taxable as ordinary income, rather than as a capital gain.

COUNSEL

Frank I. Goodman argued the cause for petitioner.
Theodore R. Colborn argued the cause for respondent.

W. PALMER DIXON et al., Petitioners,

v

UNITED STATES

381 US —, 14 L ed 2d 223, 85 S Ct 1301

Argued March 30 and 31, 1965.
Decided May 3, 1965.

Decision: Gain from sale of discounted, noninterest-bearing notes held taxable as ordinary income, rather than as capital gain, notwithstanding taxpayers' reliance at time of transaction on Commissioner's published acquiescence in Tax Court decision, interpreted by taxpayers as requiring capital gains treatment, which acquiescence was subsequently withdrawn retroactively.

SUMMARY

The instant tax refund case involved the issue whether the gain realized by taxpayers on the sale of short-term, noninterest-bearing notes which the taxpayers had purchased from the issuers at discounts, was taxable under the Internal Revenue Code of 1939 as ordinary income or as a capital gain. One of the arguments presented by the taxpayers was that in purchasing and selling the notes they had relied on the Internal Revenue Commissioner's published acquiescence in a Tax Court decision, interpreted by the taxpayers as requiring capital gains treatment of the earned original issue discount on the notes, which acquiescence was not withdrawn by the Commissioner until after the transaction by the taxpayers was closed, and that the Commissioner abused his discretion under § 7805(b) of the Internal Revenue Code of 1954 in making his subsequent published withdrawal of such acquiescence retroactive in effect. The Commissioner, who contended that the gain realized by the taxpayers was taxable as ordinary income, prevailed in the United States District Court for the Southern District of New York (224 F Supp 358), and in the Court of Appeals for the Second Circuit (333 F2d 1016).

On certiorari, the Supreme Court of the United States affirmed. In an opinion by **Brennan, J.**, expressing the unanimous view of the Court, it was held that (1) under the holding in United States v Midland Ross Corp., 14 L ed 2d 214, the earned original issue discount was taxable as ordinary income, rather than as a capital gain, (2) such result was not affected by the taxpayers' alleged reliance upon the Commissioner's published acquiescence in the Tax Court decision, and (3) the Commissioner had not abused his discretion in retroactively withdrawing his previous acquiescence.

COUNSEL

Bernard E. Brandes argued the cause for petitioners. Frank I. Goodman argued the cause for respondent.

LUCY C. SIMONS, Petitioner,

v

MIAMI BEACH FIRST NATIONAL BANK

381 US —, 14 L ed 2d 232, 85 S Ct 1315

Argued March 10, 1965.
Decided May 3, 1965.

Decision: Decision of Florida state courts that husband's ex parte Florida divorce decree extinguished nonresident wife's dower right held not to deny full faith and credit to New York separation decree, including monthly alimony, nor otherwise to violate Federal Constitution.

SUMMARY

After his wife had obtained a New York separation decree, including an award of monthly alimony, the husband moved to Florida, where he obtained a valid divorce decree in a proceeding in which his nonresident wife was served by publication only and did not make a personal appearance. After his death in Florida the wife claimed dower in proceedings for the probate of his will, and the executor opposed this claim. Thereupon she brought the instant action in the Circuit Court for Dade County, Florida, in order to set aside the divorce decree and to obtain a declaration that the divorce, even if valid to alter their marital status, did not destroy her dower claim. The action was dismissed, and the Florida District Court of Appeals for the Third Circuit affirmed. (157 So 2d 199.) The Supreme Court of Florida declined to review the case. (166 So 2d 151.)

On certiorari, the Supreme Court of the United States affirmed. In an opinion by **Brennan, J.**, expressing the views of seven members of the Court, it was held that

(1) the decisions of the Florida courts did not deny full faith and credit to the New York separation decree, and (2) the ex parte divorce decree did not violate due process by extinguishing the wife's dower right in the husband's Florida estate.

Harlan, J., concurring and joining the opinion of the Court, expressed the view that the present decision made a partial retreat from Vanderbilt v Vanderbilt, 354 US 416, 1 L ed 2d 1456, 77 S Ct 1360, holding that a wife's right to support could not be cut off by an ex parte divorce decree.

Black and **Douglas, JJ.**, likewise concurring and joining the opinion of the Court, opposed the view expressed in the concurring opinion of Mr. Justice Harlan.

Stewart and **Goldberg, JJ.**, dissented on the ground that because of lack of a federal question, the writ of certiorari should have been dismissed as improvidently granted.

COUNSEL

Robert C. Ward argued the cause for petitioner.
Marion E. Sibley argued the cause for respondent.

FEDERAL POWER COMMISSION, Petitioner,

v

UNION ELECTRIC COMPANY

381 US —, 14 L ed 2d 239, 85 S Ct 1253

Argued March 2, 1965.

Decided May 3, 1965.

Decision: Federal Power Act held to require hydroelectric power project to be licensed where it utilizes non-navigable headwaters of navigable river to generate energy for interstate power system, even if commerce on navigable waters is not significantly affected.

SUMMARY

Pursuant to § 23(b) of the Federal Power Act, an electric company filed a declaration of intention to construct a pumped-storage hydroelectric project, which was to be located on a nonnavigable tributary of a navigable river and was to provide energy for utilization in more than one state. The statute requires any person desiring to construct a dam or other project on a nonnavigable stream, but one over which Congress has jurisdiction under its authority to regulate commerce, to file a declaration of intention with the Federal Power Commission, and the statute provides that if the Commission finds that "the interests of interstate or foreign commerce would be affected by such proposed construction," the declarant may not construct or operate the project without a license. The Commission concluded that the proposed project would affect the interests of commerce and would require a license, both because the utilization of water power for the interstate transmission of electricity was contemplated and because downstream navigability would be affected. (27 FPC 801.) The Court of Appeals for the Eighth Circuit reversed, holding that the only "commerce" which was relevant to the Commission's determination was commerce on the downstream navigable river and that the project would have no significant impact on such commerce. (326 F2d 535.)

On certiorari, the United States Supreme Court reversed. In an opinion by **White, J.**, expressing the views of six members of the Court, it was held that the word "commerce" did not refer only to commerce on navigable waters, and that § 23(b) required a hydroelectric power project to be licensed where it utilized the nonnavigable headwaters of a navigable river to generate energy for an interstate power system, even if the project had no significant impact on commerce on downstream navigable waters.

Goldberg, J., joined by **Harlan** and **Stewart, JJ.**, dissented, stating that Congress intended that a license be required only where the interests of commerce on navigable waters are affected.

COUNSEL

Ralph S. Spritzer argued the cause for petitioner.
Robert J. Keefe argued the cause for respondent.

STANLEY M. CORBETT, Guardian of the
Property of Constantine Neonakis,
a Minor, Appellant,

v

VIOLA STERGIOS, etc.

381 US —, 14 L ed 2d 260, 85 S Ct 1364

Argued April 27, 1965.
Decided May 3, 1965.

Decision: 1954 Treaty of Friendship, Commerce and
Navigation between United States and Greece held
applicable to Greek national's claims to recover part
of the estate of a person deceased in Iowa.

SUMMARY

Alleging that he was an adopted child of the decedent,
the plaintiff, a minor living in Greece, instituted the
present action in an Iowa state court to recover, after
his adoptive father's death in Iowa, two-thirds of the
latter's estate. The trial court dismissed the petition.
The Supreme Court of Iowa affirmed (four of the justices
dissenting), holding that (1) there was no most-favored-
nation provision applicable to article IX of the 1954
Treaty of Friendship, Commerce and Navigation between
the United States and Greece, which permits nationals
of Greece freely to acquire property in the United States,
and (2) there was lack of reciprocity as to inheritance
rights of an adopted child. (256 Iowa 12, 126 NW2d
342.)

On appeal, the Supreme Court of the United States
reversed, in a per curiam opinion, in the light of the
Court's construction of the treaty.

COUNSEL

Robert R. Eidsmoe argued the cause for appellant.
Phillip S. Dandos argued the cause for appellee.

WATTS et al.

v

SEWARD SCHOOL BOARD et al.

381 US —, 14 L ed 2d 261, 85 S Ct 1321

May 3, 1965

Decision: Judgment of Alaska Supreme Court affirming
dismissal of teachers on grounds of "immorality"
vacated where subsequently statutory definition of
term was changed.

SUMMARY

The petitioners were dismissed from their positions as
schoolteachers in Alaska on grounds of "immorality,"
defined by the Alaska statute then in force as "conduct
of the person tending to bring the individual concerned
or the teaching profession into public disgrace or dis-
respect." Petitioners' dismissal was upheld by the Alaska
Superior Court, Third Judicial District, and affirmed by
the Alaska Supreme Court. (395 P2d 372.)

On certiorari, the United States Supreme Court, in
a per curiam opinion, vacated the judgment below and
remanded the case to the Supreme Court of Alaska, on
the ground that after the decision of the latter court
the statute had been amended so as to define "immorality"
as "the commission of an act which, under the laws of
the state, constitutes a crime involving moral turpitude."

JOHN PARROT et al., Petitioners,

v

CITY OF TALLAHASSEE, FLORIDA

381 US —, 14 L ed 2d 263, 85 S Ct 1322

May 3, 1965

Decision: State court judgment dismissing certiorari for petitioner's failure to submit certification of the record of the court below held not to rest on adequate state ground.

SUMMARY

In a per curiam opinion the Supreme Court of the United States reversed a judgment of a Florida Circuit Court and cited Robinson v Florida, 378 US 153, 12 L ed 2d 771, 84 S Ct 1693, in which it was held that the equal protection clause was violated by a Florida state conviction of Negroes and whites for remaining in a restaurant after being requested by the manager to leave.

It was also held that the judgment of the Florida District Court of Appeal, First District, which dismissed a petition for writ of certiorari for petitioner's failure to submit a certification of the Circuit Court record did not rest on an adequate independent state ground, since petitioner tried to correct the defect when notified of it, and under Florida law the defect is not jurisdictional in the sense that it cannot be corrected.

L. W. HOLT et al., Petitioners,

v

COMMONWEALTH OF VIRGINIA

381 US —, 14 L ed 2d 290, 85 S Ct 1375

Argued April 27 and 28, 1965.
Decided May 17, 1965.

Decision: Due process held violated by state convictions
of attorneys for alleging, in motions for change of
venue, bias of trial judge.

SUMMARY

In contempt proceedings instituted by a judge of the
Circuit Court of the City of Hopewell, Virginia, against
an attorney who had represented some of the defendants
in a libel suit, the attorney filed a motion requesting the
trial judge to disqualify himself from trying the contempt
case, and after denial of this motion, filed a motion for
change of venue, alleging in both motions bias on the
part of the judge. Another attorney representing the
first attorney in the contempt proceeding read this motion
to the judge as part of his argument urging a change of
venue. Both attorneys were adjudged guilty of contempt
of court, and each was fined $50. Their convictions were
affirmed by the Virginia Supreme Court of Appeals. (205
Va 332, 136 SE2d 809.)

On certiorari, the Supreme Court of the United States
reversed. In an opinion by **Black, J.,** representing the
views of eight members of the Court, it was held that
due process was violated by the contempt convictions because they were based solely on the filing of motions for
change of venue and disqualification of the trial judge
on the ground of alleged bias on his part, there being noth-

ing in the language used which would justify the convictions.

Harlan, J., dissented on the ground that the issues as to the professional propriety of the attorneys' actions involved nothing of constitutional proportions.

COUNSEL

Marvin M. Karpatkin argued the cause for petitioners. Francis C. Lee argued the cause for respondent.

UNITED STATES OF AMERICA, Plaintiff,

v

STATE OF CALIFORNIA

381 US —, 14 L ed 2d 296, 85 S Ct 1401

Argued December 7 and 8, 1964.
Decided May 17, 1965.

Decision: Grants of offshore lands to California under Submerged Lands Act of 1953 held limited to lands within 3 geographical miles of its coastline rather than lands within claimed historic boundaries.

SUMMARY

In an original action brought in 1945 in the Supreme Court of the United States, the United States sued the state of California to determine dominion over submerged lands under the 3-mile belt of sea off the California coast. The Court decreed in 1947 that the United States had full dominion over the submerged lands seaward of the ordinary low-water mark on the California coast and outside of inland waters, for 3 nautical miles seaward. (United States v California (1947) 332 US 804, 92 L ed 382, 68 S Ct 20.) A special master appointed to define the areas in greater detail filed his report in 1952, to which both parties noted exceptions. Before any further action was taken, Congress enacted the Submerged Lands Act of 1953.

In an opinion by **Harlan, J.**, expressing the views of five members of the Court, it was held that (1) regardless of a state's claimed historic boundaries, the Submerged Lands Act grants each state on the Pacific Coast only those submerged lands shoreward of a line 3 geographical miles from the seaward limit of its "inland

[Supreme Ct Sum]

waters"; (2) the term "inland waters" is to be defined in accordance with the Convention of the Territorial Sea and the Contiguous Zone as that treaty read at the time of its ratification in 1961; (3) although the Convention permits the United States to fix its international seaward boundaries either by straight base lines joining appropriate points or by the 24-mile closing rule together with the semicircle test, California was bound by the United States' election not to use the straight base-line method; and (4) under the 24-mile closing rule and the semicircle test, Monterey Bay is inland water but the other disputed areas—San Luis Obispo Bay, Santa Barbara Channel, Santa Monica Bay, San Pedro Bay, San Pedro Channel, Newport Bay, and the Gulf of Santa Catalina—are not.

Black, J., joined by Douglas, J., dissented on the ground that the Submerged Lands Act of 1953 grants to the states all submerged lands under waters within their historic state boundaries.

Warren, Ch. J., and Clark, J., did not participate.

COUNSEL

Solicitor General Archibald Cox argued the cause for plaintiff.

Richard H. Keatinge argued the cause for defendant.

George N. Hayes argued the cause for State of Alaska, amicus curiae, by special leave of Court.

MAX JABEN, Petitioner,

v

UNITED STATES

381 US —, 14 L ed 2d 345, 85 S Ct 1365

Argued March 9, 1965.   Decided May 17, 1965.

Decision: Complaint in tax prosecution held to have made required showing of probable cause, so as to entitle government to extension of period of limitations.

SUMMARY

Section 6531 of the Internal Revenue Code of 1954 provides for a 6-year period of limitations for the felony of wilfully attempting to evade federal income taxes, but also provides that where a complaint is instituted before a United States Commissioner within the 6-year period, the time shall be extended until the date which is 9 months after the date of the making of the complaint. On April 15, 1963, the day before the 6-year period was to expire, the government filed a complaint against a taxpayer charging him with wilfully filing a false return for the year 1956. The complaint, signed by a special agent of the Internal Revenue Service, described the agent's methods of investigation and stated his conclusions as to the taxpayer's attempted evasion and the amounts involved. The Commissioner determined that the complaint showed probable cause for believing that the taxpayer had committed the offense, and, at the government's request, issued a summons ordering the taxpayer to appear at a preliminary hearing on May 15, 1963. On May 11, 1963, the preliminary hearing on the complaint was continued to May 22, 1963, at the request of the United States attorney, and without objection by the taxpayer.

On May 17, 1963, the grand jury superseded the complaint procedure by returning an indictment against the taxpayer, one count of which covered the 1956 attempted evasion which the complaint had charged. Consequently, the preliminary hearing scheduled for May 22 was never held. In the United States District Court for the Western District of Missouri, the taxpayer moved to dismiss the count of the indictment pertaining to 1956, arguing that the complaint was insufficient because it did not show probable cause for believing that he had committed the offense. Both the District Court (226 F Supp 757) and the Court of Appeals for the Eighth Circuit (333 F2d 535) rejected this claim.

On certiorari, the United States Supreme Court affirmed, holding that the challenged count of the indictment was not time-barred. In an opinion by Harlan, J., expressing the views of four members of the court, it was held that (1) in order for a complaint to initiate the 9-month extension (a) the complaint must make a showing of probable cause, and (b) the government must afford the taxpayer a preliminary hearing unless the grand jury supersedes the complaint procedure by returning an indictment; and (2) the complaint had made a showing of probable cause.

White, J., joined by Black, J., concurring in the result, agreed with (2), disagreed with (1)(b), and deemed it unnecessary to consider (1)(a).

Goldberg, J., joined by Warren, Ch. J., and Douglas, J., concurring in part and dissenting in part, agreed with (1)(a) and (1)(b), but concluded that the preliminary hearing was defective because it had not been scheduled within a reasonable time, disagreed with (2), and would therefore reverse the judgment of the Court of Appeals.

COUNSEL

Morris A. Shenker argued the cause for petitioner.
Nathan Lewin argued the cause for respondent.

UNITED STATES, Petitioner,

v

ATLAS LIFE INSURANCE COMPANY

381 US —, 14 L ed 2d 358, 85 S Ct 1379

Argued March 31, 1965.   Decided May 17, 1965.

Decision: Life Insurance company held not entitled to deduct from investment income that portion of interest on nontaxable municipal bonds which was allocated to the policyholders' reserve and thus excluded from the company's taxable income.

SUMMARY

The issue in the present case was whether under the Life Insurance Company Income Tax Act of 1959 the plaintiff life insurance company was entitled to deduct from its taxable investment income that portion of interest on nontaxable municipal bonds which was allocated to the policyholders' reserve and thus excluded from the company's taxable income. Claiming that it was entitled to deduct from the total investment income both the full amount of the annual addition to reserve and the full amount of exempt interest received, and that any contrary treatment would violate the Federal Constitution, the company sued for a refund in the United States District Court for the Northern District of Oklahoma. The District Court rejected the company's claims (216 F Supp 457), but the Court of Appeals for the Tenth Circuit reversed (333 F2d 389).

On certiorari, the United States Supreme Court reversed the judgment of the Court of Appeals. In an opinion by **White, J.,** it was unanimously held that no impermissible tax on the interest earned by the company from nontaxable municipal bonds was placed by the formula prescribed in 26 USC § 804 for determining the taxable investment income of the company, under which formula investment income is divided into two parts, the policyholders' share and the company's share, and the total amount to be added to policyholder reserve is divided by the total investment yield and the resulting percentage is used to allocate each item of investment income, including tax-exempt interest, partly to the policyholders and partly to the company, the policyholders' share being excluded from taxable investment income and the remainder of each item being considered the company's share of investment income, from which the company's, but not the policyholders', share of tax-exempt interest is deductible to arrive at the taxable investment income. It was further held that, there being no statutory or constitutional barrier to the application of the formula, the exceptions provided in 26 USC §§ 804 (a)(6) and 809(b)(4), if the application of the formula results in the imposition of a tax on any tax-exempt interest, were not applicable.

COUNSEL

Solicitor General Archibald Cox argued the cause for petitioner.

Norris Darrell argued the cause for respondent.

Daniel B. Goldberg argued the cause for the Attorney General of Louisiana et al., amicus curiae.

WATERMAN STEAMSHIP CORP., Petitioner,

v

UNITED STATES

381 US —, 14 L ed 2d 370, 85 S Ct 1389

Argued April 26 and 27, 1965. Decided
May 17, 1965.

Decision: Statutory sales price fixed in Merchant Ship
Sales Act held proper cost basis in computing depreciation allowable, for federal income tax purposes,
to taxpayer on vessels purchased from United States
prior to effective date of the Act.

SUMMARY

Prior to the effective date of the Merchant Ship Sales
Act of 1946, taxpayer purchased from the United States
Maritime Commission ships which were immediately
chartered back to the United States. Upon taxpayer's
application, the original sales prices were adjusted to the
substantially lower statutory sales prices at which citizens
were entitled under the Act to purchase war-built ships
from the United States. The taxpayer first took depreciation on these vessels on the assumption that its
cost was the statutory sales price. In 1959, however, the
taxpayer sued in the United States District Court for
the Southern District of Alabama for a tax refund, contending that its real cost, and therefore its basis for depreciation, was not the statutory sales price, but the
difference between the original sales price and the net
sales price adjustment credited to taxpayer under the Act.
The District Court rendered judgment for the plaintiff.
(203 F Supp 915.) The Court of Appeals for the Fifth
Circuit reversed, holding that, under the statutory
scheme, the taxpayer's real cost was the statutory sales

price, and that this therefore was its proper depreciation basis.   (330 F2d 128.)

On certiorari, the United States Supreme Court affirmed.   In an opinion by **Goldberg, J.**, the Court unanimously agreed with the Court of Appeals.

COUNSEL

John W. McConnell, Jr., argued the cause for petitioner.

Paul Bender argued the cause for respondent, pro hac vice, by special leave of Court.

FEDERAL COMMUNICATIONS COMM'N, Petitioner,

v

TAFT B. SCHREIBER et al.

381 US —, 14 L ed 2d 383, 85 S Ct 1459

Argued April 27, 1965. Decided May 24, 1965.

Decision: Federal Communications Commission held empowered to require disclosure in public hearing of evidence regarding television program producing and packaging.

SUMMARY

During an investigation of the television industry, the Federal Communications Commission's presiding officer issued a subpoena duces tecum to a vice president of a corporate producer-packager of television programs, directing him to produce at a public hearing a list of all television programs produced or packaged by the corporation. The vice president submitted a list of such productions but refused to submit a list of programs packaged by the corporation unless such information would be held in confidence as trade secrets and confidential data. The presiding officer rejected this claim, and the Commission affirmed. The United States District Court for the Southern District of California ordered the vice president to comply with the subpoena, but required that all testimony given and documents produced be held in confidence. (201 F Supp 421). The United States Court of Appeals for the Ninth Circuit affirmed on the issue of confidentiality, stating that the District Court had not abused its discretion. (329 F2d 517.)

On certiorari, the Supreme Court of the United States modified the Court of Appeals' judgment and

remanded the cause to the District Court with directions
to enforce the Commission's orders and subpoena without qualification. In an opinion by **Warren, Ch. J.**, expressing the unanimous views of the Court, it was held
that the Communications Act of 1934 authorizes the
Commission to establish standards for determining
whether to conduct an investigation publicly or privately;
that the Commission acted within its statutory authority
in adopting a rule requiring public disclosure of information gathered in investigations, except where the pro-
ponents of a request for confidential treatment demonstrate that the public interest, proper dispatch of business,
or the ends of justice would be served by nonpublic
sessions; and that the Commission did not abuse its discretion in applying the rule to deny confidentiality where
no factual showing was made that the required dis-
closures would necessarily include business secrets.

COUNSEL

John W. Douglas argued the cause for petitioner.
Allen E. Susman argued the cause for respondents.

CORLISS LAMONT, d/b/a Basic
Pamphlets, Appellant,

v

POSTMASTER GENERAL OF THE
UNITED STATES (No. 491)

JOHN F. FIXA, Individually and as Postmaster,
San Francisco, California, et al., Appellants

v

LEIF HEILBERG (No. 848)

381 US —, 14 L ed 2d 398, 85 S Ct 1493

Argued April 26, 1965. Decided May 24, 1965.

Decision: Federal statute requiring addressee of mail
from abroad containing Communist propaganda
material to request its delivery in writing, held violation of addressee's right of free speech.

SUMMARY

The validity of a federal statute requiring a request
in writing as a prerequisite to the delivery of nonsealed
mail from abroad containing Communist propaganda
material was attacked in No. 491 in the United States
District Court for the Southern District of New York and
in No. 848 in the United States District Court for the
Northern District of California, Southern Division. After
the institution of the suits each plaintiff was notified by
the post office that none of his mail would be detained.
In No. 491 a three-judge District Court dismissed the
complaint as moot. (229 F Supp 913.) In No. 848 a
like District Court reached the merits and held that the
statute was unconstitutional under the First Amendment.
(236 F Supp 405.)

On appeals, the United States Supreme Court reversed the judgment in No. 491 and affirmed that in No. 848. In an opinion by **Douglas, J.,** representing the views of seven members of the Court, it was held that the statute, as applied, violated the addressees' right of free speech.

Brennan, J., joined by **Goldberg, J.,** concurred and joined the opinion of the Court, elaborating the proposition that the right to receive publications is a right protected by the First Amendment.

Harlan, J., concurred in the judgment of the Court on the grounds set forth in the concurring opinion.

White, J., did not participate.

COUNSEL

Leonard B. Boudin argued the cause for appellant in No. 491.

Solicitor General Archibald Cox argued the cause for appellee in No. 491 and appellants in No. 848.

Marshall W. Krause argued the cause for appellee in No. 848.

MINNESOTA MINING AND MANUFACTURING CO., Petitioner,

v

NEW JERSEY WOOD FINISHING CO.

381 US —, 14 L ed 2d 405, 85 S Ct 1473

Argued April 29, 1965.   Decided May 24, 1965.

Decision: Statute of limitations on private antitrust action held tolled by institution of Federal Trade Commission proceeding.

SUMMARY

In 1961 the plaintiff commenced an action in the United States District Court for the District of New Jersey for treble damages based on the defendant's alleged violations in 1956 of the Sherman Act and the Clayton Act. The defendant moved for dismissal of the action on the ground that it was barred by the 4-year period of limitations of § 4B of the Clayton Act, but the plaintiff contended that the statute of limitations had been tolled under § 5(b) of the Clayton Act because of an antitrust proceeding filed against the defendant in 1960 by the Federal Trade Commission. Section 5(b) provides that "a civil or criminal proceeding" instituted "by the United States" to prevent, restrain, or punish violations of any of the antitrust laws suspends the running of the statute of limitations during the pendency thereof and for one year thereafter with respect to a private antitrust action based on any "matter complained of" in the suit by the United States. The District Court denied the defendant's motion to dismiss, holding that the statute of limitations had been tolled and that the action was timely filed. (216 F Supp 507.) The Court of Appeals for the Third Circuit affirmed. (332 F2d 456.)

On certiorari, the United States Supreme Court affirmed. In an opinion by **Clark, J.**, expressing the views of five members of the Court, it was held that although the tolling provision of § 5 (b) does not expressly refer to Federal Trade Commission proceedings, the statute of limitations in § 4B is tolled by Commission proceedings to the same extent and in the same circumstances as it is by Justice Department proceedings, and that since the same conduct of the defendant was involved in both the Commission's proceedings and the plaintiff's action, the plaintiff's action was based on a "matter complained of" in the Commission's proceedings, which proceedings therefore tolled the statute of limitations.

Black, J., and **Goldberg, J.**, dissented, each in a separate opinion, on the ground that the institution of Federal Trade Commission proceedings does not toll the limitation period of § 4B.

Harlan and **Stewart, JJ.**, did not participate.

COUNSEL

Sidney P. Howell, Jr., argued the cause for petitioner. Albert G. Besser argued the cause for respondent.

PAUL V. CASE, Petitioner,

v

STATE OF NEBRASKA

381 US —, 14 L ed 2d 422, 85 S Ct 1486

Argued April 28, 1965.   Decided May 24, 1965.

Decision: Judgment of Nebraska Supreme Court holding that habeas corpus was not available to a state prisoner for vindicating a claim of violation of his federal constitutional rights, vacated and case remanded, where, pending certiorari proceedings in the United States Supreme Court, state adopted a statute providing for postconviction procedure.

SUMMARY

A state prisoner's petition for habeas corpus alleging that his federal constitutional rights were violated by denying him assistance of counsel at his trial on a charge of burglary was dismissed by a Nebraska state court. The Nebraska Supreme Court affirmed on the ground that habeas corpus was not available to determine claims of this kind.   (177 Neb 404, 129 NW2d 107.)

On certiorari, the United States Supreme Court, in a per curiam opinion, vacated the judgment of the court below and remanded the cause to that court, on the ground that after certiorari had been granted by the United States Supreme Court, the Nebraska legislature enacted a statute providing a postconviction procedure.

Clark, J., apparently joining the Court's opinion, expressed, in a concurring opinion, the hope that a modern procedure for testing federal claims in the state courts would be adopted by those states which have not yet done so.

[Supreme Ct Sum]—14

Brennan, J., concurring and apparently also joining the Court's opinion, pointed out that every consideration of federalism supported the Court's conclusion to afford the Nebraska courts the opportunity to see whether the new statute was available for the hearing and determination of the prisoner's claim.

COUNSEL

Daniel J. Meador argued the cause for petitioner.

Melvin Kent Kammerlohr argued the cause for respondent.

ATLANTIC REFINING COMPANY, Petitioner,

v

FEDERAL TRADE COMMISSION (No. 292)

GOODYEAR TIRE & RUBBER
COMPANY, Petitioner,

v

FEDERAL TRADE COMMISSION (No. 296)

381 US —, 14 L ed 2d 443, 85 S Ct 1498

Argued March 30, 1965.   Decided June 1, 1965.

Decision: Order prohibiting distributor of oil products
and manufacturer of rubber products from participating in sales-commission agreements between
themselves or with others, held within power of
Federal Trade Commission.

SUMMARY

The Federal Trade Commission found that an agreement between a distributor of oil products and a manufacturer of rubber products, under which the former, on
an overall commission basis, promoted the sale of the
tires, batteries, and accessory products of the latter to
the former's wholesale outlets and retail service station
dealers was an unfair method of competition in violation
of § 5 of the Federal Trade Commission Act.   The Commission prohibited both parties from participating in
any such arrangement, whether it was made between
the parties or with other like companies.   (58 FTC 309.)
The Court of Appeals for the Seventh Circuit affirmed
the order.   (331 F2d 394.)

On writs of certiorari, the United States Supreme Court

affirmed. In an opinion by **Clark, J.**, expressing the views of six members of the Court, it was held that under the circumstances shown the order was within the power of the Commission and was sustained by the evidence.

Stewart, J., joined by **Harlan, J.**, dissented on the ground that the order enjoining the use of any sales-commission plan of distribution was not supportable.

Goldberg, J., dissented, expressing the view that the judgments below should be vacated and the cases remanded to the Commission, since the Commission had not set forth the basis for its broad orders with sufficient clarity and completeness so that they could be properly reviewed.

COUNSEL

Frederic L. Ballard, Jr., and John F. Sonnett argued the cause for petitioners.

Daniel M. Friedman argued the cause for respondent.

UNITED GAS IMPROVEMENT COMPANY, Petitioner,

v

CONTINENTAL OIL COMPANY et al. (No. 644)

FEDERAL POWER COMMISSION, Petitioner,

v

M. H. MARR et al. (No. 693)

381 US —, 14 L ed 2d 466, 85 S Ct 1517

Argued April 28, 1965.   Decided June 1, 1965.

Decision: Sales to interstate pipeline company of leases covering proven and substantially developed reserves of natural gas to be sold in interstate commerce held subject to jurisdiction of Federal Power Commission.

SUMMARY

A natural gas company which owned and operated an interstate pipeline transmission system arranged to purchase certain leasehold interests from natural gas producers who held such interests in a field of proven and substantially developed reserves of gas.   On the basis of § 1(b) of the Natural Gas Act, providing that the Act is applicable "to the sale in interstate commerce of natural gas for resale," but not "to the production or gathering of natural gas," the Federal Power Commission asserted jurisdiction over the sales of these leasehold interests and concluded that it would not be in the public interest to certificate them.   (29 FPC 249.)   The Court of Appeals for the Fifth Circuit, reversed, holding that the leases related to the production or gathering of natural gas and were thus outside the Commission's jurisdiction. (336 F2d 320.)

On certiorari, the Supreme Court of the United States reversed. In an opinion by **Harlan, J.**, expressing the views of eight members of the Court, it was held that (1) the sales of the leases were subject to the jurisdiction of the Federal Power Commission under § 1(b) of the Natural Gas Act, and (2) decisions in prior proceedings before the Commission and the Court of Appeals for the District of Columbia Circuit did not establish the law of the case so as to preclude the Commission from reconsidering its earlier position and from asserting its jurisdiction.

Douglas, J., dissented, expressing disagreement with holding (1), supra.

COUNSEL

Solicitor General Archibald Cox and William T. Coleman, Jr., argued the cause for petitioners.

David T. Searls argued the cause for respondents.

HEARNE et al.

v

SMYLIE, Governor of Idaho, et al.

381 US —, 14 L ed 2d 476, 85 S Ct 1571

Decided June 1, 1965

Decision: Appeal from order staying Idaho legislative reapportionment suit dismissed after stay order expired and legislature reapportioned itself.

SUMMARY

The Supreme Court of the United States dismissed an appeal from an order of the United States District Court for the District of Idaho staying, for 30 days after the adjournment of the 1965 session of the Idaho legislature, a suit challenging the apportionment of the legislature. In a per curiam opinion expressing the unanimous views of the Court, it was held that since the stay order had expired by its own terms, and since the legislature had adopted a new reapportionment plan, the District Court and the parties could proceed promptly with the litigation.

SCOTT et al.

v

GERMANO et al.

381 US —, 14 L ed 2d 477, 85 S Ct 1525

Decided June 1, 1965

Decision: Federal District Court order refusing to stay proceedings in legislative reapportionment case before it vacated where highest state court had declared apportionment invalid and had retained jurisdiction of its case to insure that future elections were pursuant to valid plan.

SUMMARY

After the United States District Court for the Northern District of Illinois declared invalid the apportionment of the Illinois Senate, the Supreme Court of Illinois held the composition of the Illinois Senate invalid and retained jurisdiction of the case to insure that the next election of state legislators was pursuant to a constitutionally valid plan. The United States District Court refused to stay further proceedings in the case before it.

On direct appeal, the Supreme Court of the United States vacated the District Court's order. In a per curiam opinion expressing the views of seven members of the Court, it was held that the District Court should have stayed its hand because the state judiciary had power to require valid reapportionment or to formulate a valid districting plan.

Harlan, J., concurred in the result.

Goldberg, J., did not participate.

TRAVIA et al.

v

LOMENZO et al.

381 US —, 14 L ed 2d 480, 85 S Ct 1582

Decided June 1, 1965

Decision: Motions for stay and to accelerate appeal denied as to Federal District Court order requiring state election under apportionment plan held invalid on state grounds by highest state court.

SUMMARY

Following a Supreme Court decision holding invalid the apportionment of the New York Legislature (377 US 633, 12 L ed 2d 568, 84 S Ct 1418), the legislature adopted four alternative reapportionment plans. The United States District Court for the Southern District of New York held that three of the plans were invalid, but that one plan satisfied federal constitutional requirements. The New York Court of Appeals held all four plans invalid under the state constitution. The District Court later ordered the next legislative election to proceed under the plan which it had held valid insofar as federal constitutional standards were concerned.

The Supreme Court of the United States denied motions to stay and to accelerate the appeal from the District Court's order.

Harlan, J., dissented on the ground that the case raised serious federal questions deserving immediate argument, a prompt decision on the stay, and opinions in due course on the merits.

UNITED STATES, Petitioner,

v

ARCHIE BROWN

381 US —, 14 L ed 2d 484, 85 S Ct 1707

Argued March 29, 1965.   Decided June 7, 1965.

Decision: Section 504 of Labor-Management Reporting
and Disclosure Act of 1959, making it a crime for
a Communist Party member to serve as a union
officer or employee, held unconstitutional as a bill
of attainder.

SUMMARY

A member of a union local executive board was convicted in the United States District Court for the Northern
District of California of violating § 504 of the Labor-
Management Reporting and Disclosure Act of 1959,
which makes it a crime for a Communist Party member
to serve as a union officer or employee.   The United States
Court of Appeals for the Ninth Circuit reversed on the
ground that § 504 violates the First and Fifth Amendments to the Constitution.   (334 F2d 488.)

On certiorari, the Supreme Court of the United States
affirmed.   In an opinion by **Warren, Ch. J.,** expressing
the views of five members of the Court, it was held that
§ 504 is unconstitutional as a bill of attainder.

White, J., joined by **Clark, Harlan,** and **Stewart, JJ.,**
dissented on the ground that in view of Congress' demonstrated concern in preventing political strikes, and the
reasonableness of the means adopted to that end, § 504
is not a bill of attainder.

COUNSEL

Solicitor General Archibald Cox argued the cause for petitioner.

Richard Gladstein argued the cause for respondent.

ESTELLE T. GRISWOLD, et al., Appellants,

v

STATE OF CONNECTICUT

381 US —, 14 L ed 2d 510, 85 S Ct 1678

Argued March 29, 1965. Decided June 7, 1965.

Decision: Connecticut statute making it a criminal offense for married persons to use contraceptives held invalid as unconstitutional invasion of their privacy.

SUMMARY

A Connecticut statute made the use of contraceptives a criminal offense. The executive and medical directors of the Planned Parenthood League of Connecticut were convicted in the Circuit Court for the Sixth Circuit in New Haven, Connecticut, on a charge of having violated the statute as accessories by giving information, instruction, and advice to married persons as to the means of preventing conception. The Appellate Division of the Circuit Court affirmed and its judgment was affirmed by the Supreme Court of Errors of Connecticut. (151 Conn 544, 200 A2d 479.)

On appeal, the Supreme Court of the United States reversed. In an opinion by **Douglas, J.**, expressing the views of five members of the Court, it was held that (1) the defendants had standing to attack the statute, and (2) the statute was invalid as an unconstitutional invasion of the right of privacy of married persons.

Goldberg, J., with whom **Warren, Ch.J.**, and **Brennan, J.**, concurred, joined the opinion of the Court, elaborating in a separate opinion the view that the Fourteenth Amendment concept of liberty protects those personal rights that are fundamental, and is not confined to the specific terms of the Bill of Rights.

Harlan, J., concurred in the result, expressing the view that the statute violated basic values implicit in the concept of ordered liberty.

White, J., also concurred in the result, on the ground that the statute as applied to married couples deprived them of "liberty" without due process of law, as that concept is used in the Fourteenth Amendment.

Black and **Stewart, JJ.,** dissented in separate opinions, each joining in the other's opinion. They expressed the view that the statute violated no provision of the Federal Constitution, **Black, J.,** particularly emphasizing that there is no constitutional right of privacy.

COUNSEL

Thomas I. Emerson argued the cause for appellants. Joseph B. Clark argued the cause for appellee.

BILLIE SOL ESTES, Petitioner,

v

STATE OF TEXAS

381 US —, 14 L ed 2d 543, 85 S Ct 1628

Argued April 1, 1965.   Decided June 7, 1965.

Decision: Televising and broadcasting state criminal trial
of great notoriety held to deny due process of law
to the accused.

SUMMARY

A much publicized financier was convicted in the District Court for the Seventh Judicial District of Texas at Tyler of the offense of swindling, after a trial of great notoriety which was televised and broadcast over his objection.   The Texas Court of Criminal Appeals affirmed.   (— Tex Crim App —, — SW2d —.)

On certiorari, the Supreme Court of the United States reversed.   In an opinion by Clark, J., expressing the views of five members of the Court, it was held that in view of the great notoriety of the trial, due process of law was denied the accused by the televising and broadcasting of the proceedings.

Warren, Ch. J., with Douglas and Goldberg, JJ., joined in the Court's opinion but filed a separate opinion stating that it violates the Sixth Amendment for federal courts and the Fourteenth Amendment for state courts to allow criminal trials to be televised to the public at large.

Harlan, J., concurred in the Court's opinion subject to the reservation that the case dealt with a criminal trial of great notoriety and not with one of a more or less routine nature.

Stewart, J., joined by **Black, Brennan,** and **White, JJ.,** dissented on the ground that the televising of the accused's trial did not violate his constitutional rights.

White, J., joined by **Brennan, J.,** filed a separate dissenting opinion stating that it was premature to promulgate a flat ban on the use of cameras in the courtroom.

Brennan, J., emphasized in a separate memorandum that only four of the majority viewed televised criminal trials as constitutionally infirm, whatever the circumstances.

COUNSEL

John D. Cofer and Hume Cofer argued the cause for petitioner.

Waggoner Carr and Leon Jaworski argued the cause for respondent.

––––––––––––––

VICTOR LINKLETTER, Petitioner,

v

VICTOR G. WALKER, Warden

381 US —, 14 L ed 2d 601, 85 S Ct 1731

Argued March 11, 1965.   Decided June 7, 1965.

Decision: Rule of Mapp v Ohio, excluding in state criminal trials evidence seized in violation of the Fourth Amendment, held not to operate retrospectively upon cases finally decided prior to Mapp.

SUMMARY

After announcement of the decision of the United States Supreme Court in Mapp v Ohio (1961) 367 US 643, 6 L ed 2d 1081, 81 S Ct 1084, requiring exclusion, in state criminal trials, of evidence seized in violation of the search and seizure provisions of the Fourth Amendment, a state prisoner whose judgment of conviction had become final prior to the Mapp Case, in the sense that the availability of appeal had been exhausted and the time for petition for certiorari had elapsed, attacked the judgment by habeas corpus proceedings in the United States District Court for the Eastern District of Louisiana, on the ground that evidence used against him at his trial was obtained by unlawful search and seizure. The District Court dismissed the writ and the Court of Appeals for the Fifth Circuit affirmed. (323 F2d 11.)

On certiorari, the United States Supreme Court affirmed. In an opinion by Clark, J., expressing the views of seven members of the Court, it was held that the Mapp rule did not operate retrospectively upon cases finally decided prior to the Mapp Case.

Black and **Douglas, JJ.,** dissented, expressing the view

that the Mapp rule should apply to unconstitutional convictions which have resulted in persons being presently in
prison.

COUNSEL

Euel A. Screws, Jr., argued the cause for petitioner.
Teddy W. Airhart, Jr., argued the cause for respondent.
H. Richard Uviller argued the cause for National Dis-
trict Attorneys' Association, amicus curiae.

GEORGE ANGELET, Petitioner,

v

EDWARD M. FAY, Warden

381 US —, 14 L ed 2d 623, 85 S Ct 1750

Argued March 11, 1965. Decided June 7, 1965.

Decision: Rule against retroactive operation, upon cases finally decided prior to Mapp v Ohio, of requirement of excluding, in state criminal trial, evidence obtained by unlawful search and seizure, held applicable even though federal agents participated in the search.

SUMMARY

This is a companion case to Linkletter v Walker, supra, p. 224. Petitioner was convicted of a narcotic offense in the state courts of New York in 1951, and in 1961 by habeas corpus proceedings instituted in the United States District Court for the Southern District of New York, attacked his conviction on the ground that evidence obtained in violation of the Fourth Amendment was used against him. His application was denied by the District Court, and the Court of Appeals for the Second Circuit affirmed. (333 F2d 12.)

On certiorari, the United States Supreme Court affirmed. In an opinion by **Clark, J.**, expressing the views of seven members of the Court, it was held that the rule denying retrospective operation, upon cases finally decided prior to Mapp v Ohio, of the requirement of excluding, in state criminal trials, evidence obtained in violation of the Fourth Amendment, was applicable even though federal agents participated in the search and seizure.

Black and **Douglas, JJ.**, would reverse the judgment of the Court of Appeals for the reason stated in their dissenting opinion in Linkletter v Walker, supra, p. 224.

COUNSEL

Leon B. Polsky argued the cause for petitioner.
Gray Thoron argued the cause for respondent.
Michael Juviler argued the cause for National District Attorneys' Association, amicus curiae.

UNITED MINE WORKERS OF AMERICA,
Petitioner,

v

JAMES M. PENNINGTON et al.

381 US —, 14 L ed 2d 626, 85 S Ct 1585

Argued January 27, 1965.   Decided June 7, 1965.

Decision: Union held to forfeit exemption from antitrust
laws by agreeing with one set of employers to impose a certain wage scale on other employers.

SUMMARY

In a suit in the United States District Court for the
Eastern District of Tennessee by the trustee of a union
welfare and retirement fund against a coal company for
failure to make royalty payments under a national agreement, the coal company filed a cross claim against the
union for alleged conspiracy in violation of the antitrust
laws, partly by agreeing with the larger coal companies
to impose the terms of the agreement on all coal operators, regardless of their ability to pay.   After a jury
verdict against the union, the court overruled the union's
motion for judgment notwithstanding the verdict or in
the alternative for a new trial.   The United States Court
of Appeals for the Sixth Circuit affirmed.   (325 F2d
804.)

On certiorari, the Supreme Court of the United States
reversed.   In an opinion by **White, J.**, expressing the views
of six members of the Court, it was held that while the
union was not exempt from the antitrust laws for entering into an agreement with the large coal operators to
secure uniform labor standards throughout the industry,
the trial court erred in its jury instructions regarding

joint efforts by the union and the large operators to influence the Secretary of Labor with respect to coal purchases by the Tennessee Valley Authority.

Douglas, J., joined by **Black** and **Clark, JJ.,** concurred in the Court's opinion, interpreting it as holding that a union violates the antitrust laws by entering into an industrywide collective bargaining agreement for the purpose of forcing some employers out of business because of their inability to meet the wage scale.

Goldberg, J., joined by **Harlan** and **Stewart, JJ.,** concurred in the reversal but dissented from the opinion on the ground that collective bargaining activity concerning mandatory subjects of bargaining under the National Labor Relations Act is not subject to the antitrust laws.

COUNSEL

Harrison Combs argued the cause for petitioner.
John A. Rowntree argued the cause for respondents.
Theodore J. St. Antoine argued the cause for American Federation of Labor and Congress of Industrial Organizations, amicus curiae.

LOCAL UNION NO. 189, AMALGAMATED
MEAT CUTTERS, AND BUTCHER WORK-
MEN OF NORTH AMERICA, AFL–CIO,
et al., Petitioners,

v

JEWEL TEA COMPANY, Inc.

381 US —, 14 L ed 2d 640, 85 S Ct 1596

Argued January 27 and 28, 1965. Decided
June 7, 1965.

Decision: Union-management agreement fixing hours of
business held not violative of antitrust laws.

SUMMARY

Local unions representing virtually all the butchers in
the Chicago area agreed with a trade association of
Chicago food retailers that food store meat departments
would be open only from 9 a.m. to 6 p.m., Monday
through Saturday. Faced with a strike unless it agreed
to such terms, an employer signed the contract and then
sued the union and the association in the United States
District Court for the Northern District of Illinois, seeking invalidation under the Sherman Act of the marketing-
hours provision. The trial court dismissed the complaints
on findings that the union had imposed the marketing
hours limitation to serve their own interests in shortening
working hours and preventing butchers' work from being
done by unskilled laborers. The United States Court of
Appeals for the Seventh Circuit reversed, without disturbing the trial court's findings, concluding that a conspiracy in restraint of trade had been shown. (331 F2d
547.)

On certiorari, the Supreme Court of the United States
reversed, but could not agree on an opinion.

White, J., joined by **Warren, Ch. J.**, and **Brennan, J.**, stated that the unions did not violate the antitrust laws, because the marketing-hours restriction was so intimately related to wages, hours, and working conditions that the bona fide, arm's-length bargaining for such a provision, not in combination with a nonlabor group, was exempt from the Sherman Act.

Goldberg, J., joined by **Harlan** and **Stewart, JJ.**, concurring in the reversal, stated that collective bargaining activity concerning mandatory subjects of bargaining under the National Labor Relations Act is not subject to the antitrust laws.

Douglas, J., joined by **Black** and **Clark, JJ.**, dissented on the grounds that the agreement was not exempt from the antitrust laws.

COUNSEL

Bernard Dunau argued the cause for petitioners.
George B. Christensen argued the cause for respondent.
Solicitor General Archibald Cox argued the cause for the United States, amicus curiae, by special leave of Court.

GLOSSARY OF COMMON LEGAL TERMS

Abatement
The extinguishment of a lawsuit.

Action
A lawsuit.

Administrative determination
A decision by a government board, agency or official, rather than by a court.

Administrator
One appointed by a court to settle the estate of a deceased person. The feminine form is "administratrix."

Admiralty
The body of law governing maritime cases.

Affidavit
A sworn written statement.

Agency shop
A union-management arrangement whereby nonunion workers are employable provided that they pay to the union sums equivalent to union initiation fees and dues.

Amicus curiae
One who, not being a party to a lawsuit, assists the court in deciding the case.

Antitrust laws
Laws prohibiting restrictions on competition.

Appealable
That which may be taken to a higher court for review.

Appellant

One who appeals to a superior court from the order of an inferior court.

Appellee

A party against whom a case is appealed from an inferior court to a superior court.

Arbitration

The submission of a dispute to a selected person—not a court—for decision.

Arraign

To call a person before a judge or commissioner to answer criminal charges made against him.

Array

The whole body of persons, summoned to attend court, from whom a jury will be selected.

Assignee

One to whom property or a right is transferred.

Assignor

The transferor of property or a right.

Bareboat charter

The charter of a ship whereby the party hiring the ship must furnish the crew.

Barratry

The habitual stirring up of lawsuits.

Brief

A written legal argument submitted to the court deciding the case.

Calendar

A list of cases awaiting decision in a court.

Capital crime

An offense punishable by death.

Cause of action
A right to legal redress.

Cease-and-desist order
An order to stop doing specified acts.

Certiorari
A superior court's order to a lower court to send up the record of a case for review by the superior court.

Charter
An agreement for the hire of a ship.

Choice of remedies
An election of which form of legal redress to seek.

Civil
Not criminal, as a civil lawsuit.

Class action
A lawsuit on behalf of persons too numerous to participate actively therein.

Collapsible corporation
A corporation used to give the appearance of a long-term investment to what is actually a mere venture in the manufacture, production or construction of property, with the intention of having the profits of the venture taxed as a capital gain rather than as income.

Coram nobis
A means of challenging a court's judgment, especially in criminal cases.

Commerce clause
The provision of the United States Constitution giving Congress power to regulate commerce with foreign nations, among the states.

Common law
The body of the law apart from constitutions, treaties, statutes, ordinances, and regulations.

Condemnee
One whose property is condemned.

Condemnor
One who condemns property.

Continuance
A postponement of proceedings.

Copyright
The exclusive privilege of publishing literary or artistic productions.

Court of appeals
See United States Court of Appeals.

Cross appeal
An appeal filed by the person against whom an appeal is taken.

Cross-licensing agreement
An agreement between patent owners licensing each to use the other's patent.

De novo
Anew or over again, such as a trial de novo.

Devise
A will provision making a gift of land.

Disputes clause
A provision in a government contract for the settlement of disputes between the contractor and the government by decision of a government board or official.

District court
A federal trial court.

Diversity case
A case decided by a federal court because the parties are citizens of different states.

Double jeopardy
Placing a person twice in jeopardy of conviction for the same offense.

En banc
With all the judges of the court sitting.

Entrapment
Inducing one to commit a crime not contemplated by him for the purpose of prosecuting him.

Equal protection
The guaranty of the United States Constitution that no person or class of persons shall be denied the same protection of the laws that is enjoyed by other persons or classes of persons in like circumstances.

Establishment clause
The provision of the United States Constitution that Congress shall make no law respecting an establishment of religion.

Federal district court
See District court.

Federal question jurisdiction
The jurisdiction of federal courts over cases presenting questions of federal law.

Felony
A crime punishable by death or by imprisonment in a state prison.

Felony murder
A homicide by a person engaged in the commission of a felony.

Forma pauperis
Without the payment of legal fees in advance.

Full faith and credit clause

The provision of the United States Constitution that full faith and credit shall be given in each state to the public acts, records, and judicial proceedings of every other state.

Habeas corpus

A judicial inquiry into the legality of the restraint of a person.

Habeas corpus ad testificandum

A procedure for moving a prisoner so that he may testify in court.

Indictment

A grand jury's accusation of crime.

Interlocutory

That which settles an intervening matter but does not decide a case.

Intestate

One who dies without leaving a valid will.

Jurisdiction of subject matter

The power to decide a certain type of case.

Laches

Delay barring the right to special forms of relief.

Legatee

One to whom personal property is given by will.

Lessee

A tenant.

Lessor

A landlord.

Libel

Written defamation; in maritime cases, a suit in court.

Lien
A charge upon property for the payment of a debt.

Local action
A lawsuit, especially one involving rights to land, which can be brought only in the place where the wrong was committed.

Maintenance
Officious intermeddling in a lawsuit by assisting one party, especially by the payment of money, to prosecute or defend, particularly where the profits of the lawsuit are to be divided.

Maintenance and cure
The legal duty of a seaman's employer to care for him during his illness.

Mandamus
A judicial command to perform an official duty.

Misdemeanor
Any crime not punishable by death or by imprisonment in a state prison.

Per curiam
By the court as a whole.

Per se
By itself.

Plaintiff
A person who brings a lawsuit.

Plenary
Full or complete.

Police power
The power inherent in the states as sovereigns and not derived under any written constitution.

Privileges and immunities clause
The provision of the United States Constitution that no state shall make or enforce any law which abridges the privileges or immunities of citizens of the United States.

Pro hac vice
For this occasion.

Pro se
For himself; in his own behalf.

Proximate cause
The immediate cause of injury.

Public defender
A lawyer employed by the public to defend persons accused of crime.

Quantum meruit
The reasonable value of services.

Recidivist
One charged with a crime similar to that for which he was previously convicted.

Recognizance
A bail bond.

Remand
To order to be sent back.

Res judicata
The doctrine that a final judgment is binding on the parties to the lawsuit and the matter cannot be relitigated.

Respondent
The defendant in an action; with regard to appeals, the party against whom the appeal is taken.

Sanction
The penalty to be incurred by a wrongdoer.

Saving clause

A statutory provision preserving rights which would otherwise be annihilated by the statute.

Seaworthy

The reasonable fitness of a vessel to perform the service which she has undertaken to perform.

Statute of frauds

A statute rendering certain types of contracts unenforceable unless in writing.

Statute of limitations

A statute fixing a period of time within which certain types of lawsuits or criminal prosecutions must be begun.

Subpoena

Legal process to require the attendance of a witness.

Subrogate

To substitute one person for another with respect to certain rights.

Subrogee

One who is substituted for another so as to gain the benefit of the latter's rights.

Substantial federal question

A question of federal law of sufficient merit to warrant decision of the case by a federal court.

Substantive offense

An offense which is complete in itself and does not depend on the establishment of another offense.

Summary judgment

A judgment without a trial.

Supremacy clause

The provision of the United States Constitution that the Constitution, federal laws enacted pursuant thereto, and federal treaties shall be the supreme law of the land, binding the judges in every state, notwithstanding any state law to the contrary.

Surety

One who binds himself with another, called the principal, for the performance of an obligation with respect to which the principal is already bound and primarily liable.

Surrogate

The judge of a court dealing largely with wills and decedents' estates.

Transitory action

An action which may be brought wherever the defendant may be served with process.

Trespass

An injury intentionally inflicted on the person or property of another.

Trier of fact

One who decides questions of fact.

United States Code

The official compilation of statutes enacted by Congress.

United States Court of Appeals

The intermediate level of federal courts above the United States District Courts but below the Supreme Court of the United States.

United States District Court

See District Court.

[Supreme Ct Sum]

Unseaworthy
See Seaworthy.

USC
See United States Code.

Venue
The place where a case may be tried.

Writ of certiorari
See Certiorari.

Writ of error coram nobis
See Coram Nobis.

•

TABLE OF CASES

INDEX

ABANDONED PROPERTY
Unclaimed debts, which state may escheat, **81**

ACCESSORIES
Unfair competition by sales-commission agreement of oil products distributor and rubber products manufacturer for promotion of sale of, 211

ACCIDENT INSURANCE
Federal estate tax, flight insurance proceeds as includible in insured's estate, 170

ACCOMPLICES
Confronting witnesses, reading confession of accomplice who invoked privilege against self-incrimination as violating right of, 134

ACCUSED
Rights of, generally. Criminal Law (this index)

ADOPTION OF CHILDREN
Divorced parent's right to notice of proceeding for, 154
Greek national adopted child's right to estate of adoptive parent residing in United States, 188

ADMINISTRATORS
Decedents' Estates (this index)

ADVERTISING
Shaving cream, false advertising by use of sand covered plexiglass in television demonstration of, 130

AFFIDAVITS
Search warrant, sufficiency of affidavit for, 99

AGREEMENTS
Contracts (this index)

[Supreme Ct Sum]—17

CIVIL RIGHTS—Continued

Constitutionality of public accommodation sections of Civil Rights Act of 1964, 32, 35

Criminal statute against white person and Negro of opposite sexes living in same room as violating equal protection clause, 25

Federal injunction against threatened state prosecution to discourage civil rights activities, 146

Jury, racial discrimination in selection of, criminal cases, 113

Obstructing public passages, civil rights demonstration as, 68

Picketing before courthouse, 68, 71

Trespass convictions for demonstrations as invalidated by Civil Rights Act of 1964, 37, 83

Voters and Voting (this index)

CLAIMS AGAINST UNITED STATES

Federal Tort Claims Act, civilian and military member of National Guard as employee of United States within, 178

CLAYTON ACT

Antitrust laws, generally. Restraint of Trade (this index)

CLEARINGHOUSE SLIPS

Unlawful search, slips obtained by, admissibility in evidence, 13

CLOSING

Unfair labor practices—

employer's closing of business, 117

temporary shutdown and layoffs to support bargaining position, 122

COAL

Antitrust violation by miners' collective bargaining agreement with one set of employers to impose certain wage scale on other employers, 228

Income taxes, lessee or contract coal miners as entitled to depletion deduction, 165

COERCION

Trial judge's statement that jury must reach verdict, criminal cases, 140

[Supreme Ct Sum]

COHABITATION

Criminal statute against white person and Negro of opposite sexes living in same room as violating equal protection clause, 25

COLLECTIVE BARGAINING

Air Carriers (this index)

Antitrust violations—

hours of business, agreement fixing, 230

wage scale, agreement with one set of employers to impose on other employers, 228

Contracting out maintenance work as subject of mandatory bargaining, 27

Exhaustion of collective bargaining grievance procedures as prerequisite to action for severance pay, 77

Extent of unionization as factor in determining appropriate bargaining unit, 138

Unfair labor practices—

lockout and employing temporary replacement by nonstruck members of multiemployer bargaining group, 120

temporary shutdown and layoffs to support bargaining position, 122

COLORED PERSONS

Civil Rights (this index)

Criminal statute against white and colored persons of opposite sexes living in same room as violating equal protection clause, 25

COMMENT

By counsel. Argument of Counsel (this index)

By court or judge. Instructions to Jury (this index)

COMMERCE

Civil Rights Act of 1964, public accommodation sections as within commerce power, 32, 35

Excise tax on sale outside state, 142

FPC jurisdiction over gas partly resold in interstate commerce due to commingling with other gas, 46, 85

Hydroelectric project for interstate power system, license to establish on nonnavigable headwaters of navigable river, 186

COMMERCIAL PAPER

Income tax on gains from sale of discounted, noninterest-bearing notes, 180, 182

ESTOPPEL AND WAIVER
Evidence obtained by unlawful search, effect of failure to object to, 56

Jury trial, validity of requirement of court's and government's consent to accused's waiver of, 89

EVIDENCE
Federal Employers' Liability Act action, sufficiency in, 79

Inferences (this index)

Television program producing and packaging, FCC power to require disclosure in public hearing of evidence as to, 203

Unlawful search and seizure, evidence obtained by. Search and Seizure (this index)

EXAMINATION
Defendant, mental and physical examination of, under Federal Rules of Civil Procedure, 15

Voting registration examination requiring interpretation of Constitution, validity of, 101

EXCISE TAXES
Sales outside state, state excise tax on, 142

EXECUTIVE ORDERS
Oil and gas, Secretary of Interior's interpretation of executive order as not barring leases on certain public lands, effect of, 87

EXECUTORS AND ADMINISTRATORS
Decedents' Estates (this index)

EXEMPTION FROM MILITARY SERVICE
Conscientious objectors, unorthodox beliefs as to Supreme Being as affecting exemption of, 107

EXEMPTION FROM TAXATION
Income taxes—
life insurance company's deduction of interest on tax-exempt municipal bonds allocated to policyholders' reserve, 199
transfer of business to tax-exempt foundation as sale for purposes of, 158

EXHAUSTION OF REMEDIES
Severance pay, exhaustion of collective bargaining grievance procedures as prerequisite to action for, 77

HOLDING COMPANIES
Jurisdiction as to plan to create new national banks operated by bank holding company, 51

HOMICIDE
Assault With Intent to Murder (this index)
Comment by counsel or court on accused's failure to testify at state prosecution, 163
Jurors associating with deputy sheriff prosecution witnesses as violating due process, 59

HOPS
Patents incorporated in hop picking machines, royalties after expiration of, 3

HOURS OF BUSINESS
Collective bargaining contract fixing, 230

HUSBAND AND WIFE
Contraceptives, validity of law prohibiting use of, 220
Divorce and Separation (this index)

HYDROELECTRIC PROJECT
License to establish project for interstate power system on non-navigable headwaters of navigable river, 186

IDAHO
Apportionment of legislature, dismissal of appeal from stay of suit challenging, 215

ILLINOIS
Apportionment of legislature, state courts' powers as to, 216

IMPAIRMENT OF CONTRACTS
Application to previous land sales of statute requiring exercise within five years after forfeiture of lands for nonpayment of interest of right to reinstatement from forfeiture as violating prohibition against, 66

IMMORALITY
Dismissal of teachers for, subsequent change of statutory definition of term as affecting, 190

IMMUNITY FROM SUIT
Voting rights of Negroes, suability of State under statute permitting suits by United States to protect, 103

[Supreme Ct Sum]—18

PREFERENCES AND PRIORITIES

Distributing agent in reorganization proceedings, personal liability for improper distribution impairing government's priority claim, 40

PREJUDICE

Attorney's contempt in seeking change of venue for prejudice of trial judge, 192

PRESENCE

Inference of guilt from accused's presence at illegal still, 95

PRICE

Income taxes, price fixed in Merchant Ship Sales Act as basis for depreciation on vessels purchased prior to effective date of Act, 201

PRIORITIES

Preferences and Priorities (this index)

PRIVACY

Married persons' use of contraceptives as within right of, 220

PROBABLE CAUSE

Income tax evasion prosecution, sufficiency of showing of probable cause for tolling of limitations as to, 196

Production of taxpayer's records for years barred by statute of limitations, necessity to show probable cause to suspect fraud to compel, 7, 9

Search after arrest without warrant, probable cause as affecting legality of, 13

PRODUCTION OF BOOKS AND RECORDS

Production of taxpayer's records for years barred by statute of limitations, necessity to show probable cause to suspect fraud to compel, 7, 9

PROMISSORY NOTES

Income tax on gains from sale of discounted, noninterest-bearing notes, 180, 182

PROSPECTIVE OPERATION

Retroactive Operation (this index)

PUBLIC ACCOMMODATIONS

Civil Rights Act of 1964, constitutionality of public accommodation sections of, 32, 35

PUBLIC HEARING

Television program producing and packaging, FCC power to require disclosure in public hearing of evidence as to, 203

PUBLIC LANDS

Boundaries of offshore lands granted to California under Submerged Lands Act, 194

Impairment of contracts, application to previous land sales of statute requiring exercise within five years after forfeiture of lands for nonpayment of interest of right to reinstatement from forfeiture as violating prohibition against, 66

Oil and gas, Secretary of Interior's interpretation of executive order and public land order as not barring leases on certain public lands, effect of, 87

PUBLIC OFFICERS

Libeling of, instructions to jury as to intent as affecting, 126

PURCHASES

Generally. Sales (this index)

RACE DISCRIMINATION

Civil Rights (this index)

RADIO AND TELEVISION

Criminal trial, denial of due process by televising and broadcasting, 222

Injunction against union picketing and boycott of station constituting part of integrated enterprise meeting NLRB jurisdictional standards, state court's lack of jurisdiction as to, 115

Program producing and packaging, FCC power to require disclosure in public hearing of evidence as to, 203

Shaving cream, false advertising by use of sand covered plexiglass in television demonstration of, 130

RAILROADS

All-commodity railroad freight rates, applicability of Interstate Commerce Act § 1(6), 42

Federal Employers' Liability Act (this index)

"Substantial interest," within Clayton Act, of officers of selling corporation in purchasing corporation, 105

RAILWAY LABOR ACT

Air carriers, collective bargaining by, generally. Air Carriers (this index)

RESERVATIONS

Income of trading post company from sales to Indians on, invalidity of state tax on, 172

RESIDENCE

Domicil and Residence (this index)

RESTAURANTS

Public accommodation sections of Civil Rights Act of 1964, constitutionality of, 35

Trespass convictions for demonstrations as invalidated by Civil Rights Act of 1964, 37, 83

RESTRAINT OF TRADE

Collective bargaining as affected by antitrust laws. Collective Bargaining (this index)

Dehydrated onion and garlic market, 161

"Substantial interest," within Clayton Act, of officers of selling corporation in purchasing corporation, 105

Tolling of limitations on private antitrust action by FTC proceedings, 207

RETROACTIVE OPERATION

Evidence obtained by unlawful search and seizure, rule against use in state courts, 224, 226

Impairment of contracts, application to previous land sales of statute requiring exercise within five years after forfeiture of lands for nonpayment of interest of right to reinstatement from forfeiture as violating prohibition against, 66

Trespass convictions for demonstrations as invalidated by Civil Rights Act of 1964, 37, 83

RIVERS

Hydroelectric project for interstate power system, license to establish on nonnavigable headwaters of navigable river, 186

ROBBERY

Coercive effect of trial judge's statement that jury must reach verdict, 140

Confronting witnesses, right of, in state prosecution, 132, 134

ROYALTIES

Patents incorporated in machines sold, royalties after expiration of, 3

RUBBER PRODUCTS

Unfair competition by sales-commission agreement of oil products distributor and rubber products manufacturer, 211

SALES

District of Columbia Income and Franchise Tax Act, propriety of apportionment formula based on sales factor under, 156

Excise tax on sales outside state, 142

Gas lease, FPC jurisdiction as to sale to pipeline company, 213

Gas partly resold due to commingling with other gas, FPC jurisdiction over, 46, 85

Income Taxes (this index)

Indians on reservation, invalidity of state tax on trading post company's income from sales to, 172

"Substantial interest," within Clayton Act, of officers of selling corporation in purchasing corporation, 105

Unfair competition by sales-commission agreement of oil products distributor and rubber products manufacturer for promotion of sale of tires, batteries, and accessories, 211

SANDPAPER

Shaving cream, false advertising by use of sand covered plexiglass as sandpaper in television demonstration of, 130

SATURDAY

Drowning during outing on, as arising out of and in course of employment, 128

SAUDI ARABIA

Expenses for transportation of witnesses from Saudi Arabia to New York, allowance of, 29

SCHOOLTEACHERS

Dismissal for immorality as affected by subsequent change of statutory definition of term, 190

SEAMAN

Jones Act as precluding recovery for seaman's death in territorial waters due to unseaworthiness, 21

SEARCH AND SEIZURE

Affidavit for search warrant, sufficiency of, 99

Communist Party and its operations, invalidity of search warrant for all literary material concerning, 61

[Supreme Ct Sum]—19

[Supreme Ct Sum]

SHAVING CREAM

False advertising in use of sand covered plexiglass in television demonstration of, 130

SHERIFF

Jurors associating with deputy sheriff prosecution witnesses as violating due process, 59

SHERMAN ACT

Antitrust laws, generally. Restraint of Trade (this index)

SHIPS AND SHIPPING

Income taxes, price fixed in Merchant Ship Sales Act as basis for depreciation on vessels purchased prior to effective date of Act, 201

Jones Act as precluding recovery for seaman's death in territorial waters due to unseaworthiness, 21

SHUTDOWN

Closing (this index)

SIT-IN DEMONSTRATIONS

Trespass convictions for sit-in demonstrations as invalidated by Civil Rights Act of 1964, 37

SLANDER

Libel and Slander (this index)

SOLDIERS

Armed Forces (this index)

SOUTH KOREA

Drowning during Saturday outing in, as arising out of and in course of employment, 128

STATE

Unclaimed debts, which state may escheat, 81

Voting rights of Negroes, suability under statute permitting suits by United States to protect, 103

STATE DEPARTMENT

Passports for travel in Cuba, refusal of, 176

STATE INSTITUTIONS

Support of mentally ill persons in, validity of statute imposing liability on estate or relatives for, 110

WRONGFUL DEATH

Jones Act as precluding recovery for seaman's death in territorial waters due to unseaworthiness, 21

ZONING

Airports, height limitation of structures in vicinity of, 63